PRAIRIE STATE BOOKS

You Know Me Al

YOU KNOW ME AL

RING W. LARDNER

Introduction by Mark Harris

UNIVERSITY OF ILLINOIS PRESS
Urbana and Chicago

Introduction ©1992 by the Board of Trustees of the University of Illinois
Manufactured in the United States of America
P   5   4   3   2   1

This book is printed on acid-free paper.

Library of Congress Cataloging-in-Publication Data

Lardner, Ring W., 1885-1933.
    You know me Al / Ring W. Lardner : Introduction by Mark Harris.
        p.   cm. — (Prairie State books)
    Originally composed as a series of six selections for the Saturday
evening post, Mar. 7-Nov. 7, 1914.
    ISBN 0-252-06230-2 (pbk. : alk. paper)
    I. Title.   II. Series.
PS3523.A7Y6   1992b
813'.52—dc20   91-18858
                                                              CIP

CONTENTS

INTRODUCTION

You Know Me Al was Ring Lardner's first pub-
lished book of fiction and his only novel, if we may
call a book a novel whose author never intended it
to be one.

These "busher's letters" had been composed as
a series of six selections for the *Saturday Evening
Post* between March 7 and November 7, 1914, when
Lardner was a twenty-nine-year-old columnist for
the *Chicago Tribune.*

At this time, he had also begun to produce sons.
Lardner's discovery of himself as father seems to
me to be central to the direction of *You Know Me
Al,* for Lardner, I think, was above all father, in
contradiction to half a century of literary gossip
tending to preserve him mainly as one of the thirsty
wits of the Algonquin.

Lardner was the liberator of his sons, each of
whom traveled a liberal, independent way as writer
and citizen. In this Lardner's wife was his wholly
supportive partner. She was the former Ellis Abbott,

of a prosperous Indiana family, and had graduated with honors from Smith College. Three of their sons—John, James, and Ring Jr.—were born between 1912 and 1915; their fourth son, David, was born in 1919.

The *Saturday Evening Post* series appeared as a book in 1916, at a time when Lardner's breadwinning work was principally his column "In the Wake of the News." He had come to his column after years as a sports reporter, mainly for the *Tribune* and the *Chicago Examiner.* His memorable task had been to follow the city's baseball teams, the Cubs and the White Sox, from park to park and city to city to report their welfare to the folks at "home," although there were then, as now, few enough baseball players whose homes were located in the cities whose baseball shirts they wore.

"Almost as soon as the *Post* began to publish them," Lardner's son John wrote in 1959, "the letters made their author as famous as the President of the United States. (They were to keep him famous in the same degree throughout the next two or three administrations.)"

John Lardner has also told us something of his father's intention for *You Know Me Al:* "The busher letters were not written with artistic prestige in mind. They were written because there was an urgent need around the house of the two hundred dollars each of the first installments brought from *The Saturday Evening Post.*"

Who am I to quibble with the family? But John was two years old the year the series appeared in the *Saturday Evening Post* and may not have known the whole story. Granted a basis of economic need, the busher's letters nevertheless arose from Lardner's view of the world, his impressions of life as he had seen it. If he produced a novel he had never intended, a book of commitment and conviction, he did it in spite of his having consciously begun the tale in the interest only of money. He refused to be, said his son John, "loose and garrulous." Rather, "the things that interested him were snugly organized. His subjects suited his special abilities. He carried a sharp knife; with one stroke of it, in *You Know Me Al,* he laid bare all the vital parts."

Lardner had begun to publish at age sixteen with a poem in the *Niles Daily Star,* June 14, 1901, in Niles, Michigan, where he was born. The poem commemorates Lardner's high-school graduation in twenty quatrains in a style he would frequently parody. His lead-off stanza was this:

Up Learning's ladder, round by round
We've climbed with many a fall:

But, through the toil, companionship
Has made amends for all.

After high school Lardner conveyed himself from Niles ten miles across the line to South Bend, Indiana, where he wrote for two years for the *South Bend Times;* thence to Chicago to the *Chicago Inter-Ocean* and the *Chicago Examiner;* and finally, in 1908, to the *Tribune,* to the ball parks, hotels, and railroads.

During the twenties, no longer a reporter, Lardner supported himself and his family at a high level of affluence by writing short fiction for popular magazines, with a syndicated column, a syndicated comic strip, periodical articles, and with occasional work, not especially profitable, as a songwriter and as a contributor to stage plays and motion pictures.

Fame never tempted Lardner. He neither sought it nor worshipped it nor admired the men or women who had won it. In this he strikes me as significantly different from many writers then and now who cared too much for renown, and who ruined themselves in pursuit of it. I think especially of those Illinois writers whose careers I have followed with more than passing interest—Vachel Lindsay, Sandburg, Hemingway, for example—who may sometimes have confused themselves with their images;

who made the mistake of believing their press notices.

Lardner was skeptical. Perhaps his own newspaper experience had taught him the hollowness of public notice. He knew everything, and he seemed to know it early. He was a wise, kind, and courageous man. He knew what mattered. The future of his reputation was of little interest to him. He kept no record of himself. "My God!" Fitzgerald wrote in 1933 when Lardner died, "he hadn't even saved [his stories]—the material of 'How to Write Short Stories' was obtained by photographing old issues of magazines in the public library."

"Did you ever write out a biographical sketch?" his illustrious editor Maxwell Perkins asked Lardner in 1925, neither for the first time nor the last. "We need one badly for our agents, etc. Anything you may have we could, I imagine, adjust, and if you have nothing couldn't you run something off?" Lardner ran off one book of "autobiography" called *The Story of a Wonder Man* (most of which had appeared in his weekly column), but paragraph 1 of chapter 1 is as close as he could come to the idea of a factual record of himself:

The first week in March, 1885, was a gala week throughout the civilized world, the United States in general and the latter's great middle west in particular. In this one week there was an unfounded rumor of a royal betrothal between Queen Victoria and King Gillette; a young Washington dentist, Dr. Ghoul, watched a mixed fivesome tee off at Chevy Chase and predicted that four of them would hàve pyorrhea; the Lardners of Niles, Mich., announced the birth of a fourteen pound man child, and almost on the same date twenty-nine years later, or maybe it was 28th of June, the Archduke Ferdinand was shot down at Sarajevo.

These events occurred before there were telephones or telegraphs and the news of the Lardner boy's birth had to be flashed to the world by runners. Sparing no expense, the parents hired Paavo Nurmi to notify distant relatives and engaged Charlie Paddock for the sprints. In less than two weeks the Niles post office began to be flooded with letters of all kinds, most of them being circulars from strangers advocating the installation of an oil heater. "They pay for themselves in what you save on coal," was the general gist.

"There were no files in my father's workroom," Ring Lardner, Jr., wrote in a foreword to a book of collected letters. "One thing you can be sure of in my father's case is that he didn't dream you or any other third party would ever read these words of his. It never even occurred to him, when he started selling short stories, that they would survive their issues of the SATURDAY EVENING POST."

There's a rich comedy of cross-purposes in Lardner's correspondence with Maxwell Perkins, the renowned editor at Charles Scribner's Sons who had in significant ways brought along or was soon to bring along other authors from youth and anonymity to public success. Those whose names we know best are Fitzgerald, Hemingway, and Thomas Wolfe.

It was Perkins's conviction that Lardner ought to have been striving for longer works to ensure his fame; fatter books of stories; best of all, novels. "I wish though, that for the next book of stories, we could have one long one, and the longer the better," Perkins wrote to Lardner in 1926. "I know that while you are writing for the Cosmopolitan, this is impossible for periodical use but couldn't you do one long one just for a book? If it were twenty or twenty-five thousand words, we would have something entirely new, and we could make ever so much of it, and we might be able to even get a financial return that would warrant the sacrifice of magazine publication."

Lardner was not compliant. Four months later Perkins wrote to him again. "You always do everything your own way so perhaps you would rather not, but I wish I could sometime have a talk with you in the idea that you are now so much freer, that you might be willing to think of a book on a larger scale than you have done. The last thing I want to be is a nuisance, so if you would rather not, all right."

Lardner would rather not. Perkins wrote to him in October 1927, "[Scott Fitzgerald] read me from a letter of yours in which you said your play was coming on. May it be a [magnificent] success! But since it is written, and all the work done on it, I hoped you might begin to think of a book." December 20, 1927: "I do wish you would write one long short story to head a book." One year later: "And I wish there were something I could do to compel you to write that 40,000 word story, or novel, or whatever it ought to be called. I do not know of any publishing news that would be more interesting than that such a book by you was to come out." Three months afterward—perhaps forgetfully: "Aren't you doing that 40,000 word story you were telling me about?" Two months later: "If only you would do that 40,000 word story you thought of,

now would be the time for it, with the great
distribution of 'Round Up' as a background." Two
weeks later: "Have you ever begun on the long
story?" And more than a year later: "I am sorry
you have not been feeling well.—But spring is not
so far off now, and that always, I find, brings a
man up a good many notches. I wish you would
take a year off from New York, and the theatre,
etc., and quietly do a novel!"

Quietly or otherwise, Lardner never obliged his
friend Perkins. He could not write long. He knew
his distance and his limits. On the question of self-
identity he wrote in his preface to *How to Write
Short Stories,* "The answer is that you can't find
no school in operation up to date, whether it be a
general institution of learning or a school that
specializes in story writing, which can make a great
author out of a born druggist."

Once more "the first week in March," but a
century later. One hundred years from the day of
Lardner's birth I arrived at Albion College in
Albion, Michigan, a hundred miles from Niles.
Here, in the company of members of Lardner's
family, and scholars and writers and Lardner fans
from all over America, I assisted in the celebration

of the centennial of his birth. It was a Wednesday. He had died at forty-eight and now he was one hundred.

When I arrived at the college I was informed that the Lardners had driven down for the afternoon to tour Niles. But I might be seated with them for dinner if I wished. Did I wish? Indeed, I could wish for nothing more. This was why I had come, to see Lardners, as many as possible, and to live to enchant myself with the thought that on the night of the centennial of the birth of Ring Lardner I had dined with Lardners left and right. Everybody at table was a Lardner but me:

Ring Lardner, Jr., sole survivor of the four sons of Ring Lardner, who had succeeded in life with remarkable screen-writing achievements (*Woman of the Year* and *M*A*S*H,* among others), and whose noble principle it was to have chosen to go to prison for ten months in 1950-51 rather than to have peached on friends and comrades before the infamous House Un-American Activities Committee;

Frances Chaney Lardner, wife of Ring Lardner, Jr., actress, widow of her husband's brother, David, who was killed by a mine in Europe in World War II;

Kate Lardner, daughter of David and Frances,

granddaughter of Ring, film editor, writer;

Jim Lardner, son of Frances and Ring, Jr., grandson of Ring, writer for the *New Yorker;*

Natalie, wife of Jim, film editor;

Susan Lardner, daughter of John, granddaughter of Ring, writer, teacher.

Many tables were spread for the occasion, and speakers engaged. Among the speakers was a man with a glowing bald head named Jonathan Yardley, a book reviewer, author of a biography of Lardner, who I assumed was appearing here as a friendly witness since he had expressed in his book his deep indebtedness to Ring Lardner, Jr., in the following way:

> At times his courtesies astonished me; he permitted me, for example, to walk away from his house at New Milford with a large cardboard box filled with irreplaceable letters, clippings and papers that his mother had scrupulously saved. . . . He read my manuscript with great care, and corrected me on a number of errors or misinterpretations of fact. But he never once challenged my interpretations of his father's life and work, though I feel sure he disagrees with a number of them, and for this more than anything else I am grateful to him: not

merely did he give me much of the material
for this book, but he further gave me the
freedom to write it, for better or for worse, as
I felt it should be written.

But Yardley's address to us that night omitted
the gratitude he had expressed in his book. He was
apparently now persuaded, as reviewers and critics
often may be, that we in his audience sat waiting
in suspense for his version of things, in this case
his evaluation of the work of Ring Lardner.

By enunciating his opinion for us he would relieve
us of the effort of forming our own. The critic frees
us from thought. Yardley advised us how history
had come out—where Lardner ranked among the
writers of the world. Yardley was as certain of
himself as any TV person reading out the stock-
market numbers. He had captured literature by
scientific expertise, explaining good and bad to
us, high and low, repealing the venerable wisdom
that every book connects differently with every
reader.

Lardner, it turned out, according to Yardley's
soundings, ranked low in literature, low down on
the scale of things, a low-down writer. Yardley was
trying to assign a literary place to Lardner. I didn't
mind his missing the idea of the evening—celebra-

tion needn't be uncritical—but the idea he missed was that nobody in the world could establish a handicap number for Ring Lardner or for any other writer.

When Yardley was done we birthday celebrants passed to the society of the evening. Our speaker was stunned by the coolness with which he had been received. I was tempted, in the manner of Jack Keefe, to give Yardley a good punch in the jaw. Instead, I only scowled at him. My last sight of him was of his standing in a state of shock in the public entryway of the guest house where we were lodged, quite obstructing the foot traffic. Those of us coming and going softly walked around him in embarrassment.

At the time of his writing *You Know Me Al* Lardner could scarcely have imagined the scope or endurance of its future. Fame and reputation came suddenly. He had not aimed at it. He had only been writing, as far as he knew, breadwinning pieces for the *Saturday Evening Post*. Put them together, call them a novel, name the novel *You Know Me Al,* and the work oddly flourishes and endures beyond all expectations and in spite of everything that seemed reasonable to believe on the basis of its visible text.

In 1924, eight years after *You Know Me Al,* the critic Edmund Wilson delivered a blow against Ring Lardner that would echo through the years as judgment. "If Ring Lardner has anything more to give us," Wilson wrote, "the time has now come to deliver it."

But Lardner had written the book of his life. All he could deliver he had delivered. If critics or readers asked him ritual questions about the history of his book he could only respond (as he did in the briefest preface in 1925) with that old weapon of choice, his humor: "The writer has been asked frequently. . . Who is the original of Jack Keefe?". . . The original of Jack Keefe is not a ball player at all, but Jane Addams of Hull House, a former Follies girl."

Lardner's range, Fitzgerald complained, was limited to "the diameter of Frank Chance's diamond." But that was where Lardner's experience had led him. The major event of his life was his having been cast in with baseball players. They were the principal people of the world in which he had been working as a sports reporter for nearly a decade. They had delivered their powerful impact on a young man still relatively innocent of life, on the first big job of his career. Life might never again strike him so forcefully. He was awed by the players' habits, their methods, their language, and their code. These people of the world called baseball were as real and as significant and as legitimately symbolic of the general life as people anywhere in whatever writer's range.

How in the world could Lardner have said it better by saying it over again? Here comes Jack Keefe, keeping in touch by mail with his old buddy Al Blanchard back in Bedford. Jack the ballplayer has been sold by fate and Terre Haute of the Central League to the Chicago Americans, known also as White Sox. *Sold!* In those old days the profit of the sale of flesh accrued not to the player but to his "owner."

But this is Jack's only chance in life. Baseball is his only skill. We all understand that. He wants to do well and he wants to earn money for doing well. He signs with Chicago for $1,500 after vowing to friend Al that he would never take a penny less than $3,000. His pride is damaged. He will declare over and over what he will do and why, and when he fails he will explain it away. Of course these things are never Jack's fault. In his explanations he may be quite like us.

Jack does not play as well for Chicago as he had said he would play. He is to be sent down to San

Francisco. He confronts Charles Comiskey, in truth as in fiction the owner of the team. "I asked him how they got waivers on me . . ."—*how could anybody waive me away, good as I am? Or can it be that I am not as good as I think I am?* We know the feeling, and we feel for Jack, though Comiskey is less patient than we—he is a rich man and cannot afford it. "Then he patted me on the back and says Go out there and work hard boy and maybe you'll get another chance some day. . . . I ain't had no fair deal Al and I ain't going to no Frisco. I will quit the game first and take that job Charley offered me at the billiard hall."

The busher plays as well as he can for San Francisco, wins eleven consecutive games, and returns in August to Chicago. "I got here last Tuesday and set up in the stand and watched the game that afternoon. Washington was playing here and Johnson pitched. I was anxious to watch him because I had heard so much about him. Honest Al he ain't as fast as me." He pitches and wins his first comeback game. "Well the Athaletics come and I guess you know by this time what I done to them. And I had to work against Bender at that but I ain't afraid of none of them now Al."

Jack has two lady friends, not quite simultaneously. They are Violet and Hazel. Hazel asks him for money. "She asked me to send her a hundred dollars for her fare and to buy some cloths with. I sent her thirty dollars for the fare and told her she could wait till she got to Chi to buy her cloths." Jack is careful of money. Aren't we all? His stinginess exceeds anyone's we have ever known, except perhaps our own. "I guess my thirty dollars is gone," Jack writes, having heard of Hazel's ending their courtship, "because in her letter she called me a cheap skate and she inclosed one one-cent stamp and two twos and said she was paying me for the glass of beer I once bought her. I bought her more than that Al but I won't make no holler." Jack's negotiation, through Al, for the cab to meet him (or not to meet him) at the Bedford station appears to me to be a comic masterpiece of the literature of frugality.

Jack does not marry Violet, either, nor move with her to Bedford for the winter. How awful now to endure the agony of paying rent on a house he does not even occupy. But now comes Florence, and "I am a married man. Yes Al I and Florrie were married the day before yesterday just like I told you we was going to be and Al I am the happyest man in the world though I have spent $30 in the last 3 days incluseive."

The honeymoon is over. Things break down. "I

and Florrie had our first quarrle the other night."
They live enclosed with two people in an apartment
Jack had not wished to move into. Money is short.
He borrows $25 from Al, he asks for more, and he
soon becomes unable or unwilling to remember
exactly how much he borrowed. He thinks of jumping the rent.

Florence is pregnant. Baby is born. The baby,
Allen, appears to be left-handed, like Jack's antag-
onist, Allen, the left-handed pitcher with whom
Jack and Florence share an apartment. "Babys is
great stuff Al and if I was you I would not wait no
longer but would hurry up and adopt 1 somewheres."

In a remarkable and revealing sequence Jack
Keefe's concentration on his pitching is impaired
by his distraction over whether or not his baby is
ill. Lured by trickery into complacency about the
baby's health, Jack is afterward lured again into
an overseas baseball barnstorming tour from which
everyone stands to profit but him. After much
indecision he consents to sail, and on the day of
his departure he writes a last letter to Al, pleading
with his friend to care for Florence and the baby:

Here is the things I want to ask you to try
and do Al and I am not asking you to do
nothing if we get threw the trip all right but

if something happens and I should be drowned
here is what I am asking you to do for me and
that is to see that the insurence co. dont skin
Florrie out of that $1000.00 policy and see that
she all so gets that other $250.00 out of the
bank and find her some place down in Bedford
to live if she is willing to live down there
because she can live there a hole lot cheaper
than she can live in Chi and besides I know
Bertha would treat her right and help her out
all she could. All so Al I want you and Bertha
to help take care of little Al until he grows up
big enough to take care of him self and if he
looks like as if he was going to be left handed
dont let him Al but make him use his right
hand for every thing. Well Al they is 1 good
thing and that is if I get drowned Florrie won't
have to buy no lot in no cemetary and hire no
herse.

Friends and partisans of *You Know Me Al* have
cited the book's linguistic achievement, its supposed
mastery of vernacular idiom. And yet it seems to
me that the triumph of Lardner's comic prose is
something other than its exactitute in capturing
authentic colloquial language. I believe Jack Keefe's
words exist not so much in life as in the ears of

Ring Lardner, who must have laughed as he wrote them in the instant of invention, and may have been surprised to hear afterward—even from H. L. Mencken, recorder and custodian of the American language—how painstaking he had been.

Lardner's greater achievement is his projection of himself into *You Know Me Al*. Lardner, like Keefe, was the nervous young man at the threshold of career, the father, the family man, the money-worrier, all the while the invisible author. But without his presence his book would be powerless to renew itself, as it has done, from administration to administration.

I see Jack Keefe at the railing of the ship, looking a good deal like Ring Lardner. Bon voyage, Jack. (How he might have spelled it I cannot guess). When Jack's ship sails to the horizon I will remember, I think, not only the difficult, defensive, vulgar, stingy, insensitive baseball player but a man for whom the great task of life has become family and fatherhood. So it had become for Ring, who created Jack at an hour of family necessity, we are told, for two hundred dollars per installment in the *Saturday Evening Post*.

Note: Many books have been helpful to me in the preparation of this introduction. Those works which have been especially useful, and from which I have sometimes quoted directly, are *Ring Lardner: A Descriptive Bibliography,* Matthew J. Bruccoli and Richard Layman; *Letters from Ring* and *Ring Around Max,* edited by Clifford M. Caruthers; *The Lardners: My Family Remembered,* by Ring Lardner, Jr.; and John Lardner's introduction (1959) to *You Know Me Al.*

You Know Me Al

CHAPTER

1

A Busher's Letters Home

Terre Haute, Indiana, September 6.

FRIEND AL: Well, Al old pal I suppose you
seen in the paper where I been sold to the
White Sox.   Believe me Al it comes as a surprise to me and I bet it did to all you good old
pals down home.   You could of knocked me over
with a feather when the old man come up to me
and says Jack I've sold you to the Chicago Americans.

I didn't have no idea that anything like that
was coming off.   For five minutes I was just dum
and couldn't say a word.

He says We aren't getting what you are worth
but I want you to go up to that big league and
show those birds that there is a Central League

on the map. He says Go and pitch the ball you been pitching down here and there won't be nothing to it. He says All you need is the nerve and Walsh or no one else won't have nothing on you.

So I says I would do the best I could and I thanked him for the treatment I got in Terre Haute. They always was good to me here and though I did more than my share I always felt that my work was appresiated. We are finishing second and I done most of it. I can't help but be proud of my first year's record in professional baseball and you know I am not boasting when I say that Al.

Well Al it will seem funny to be up there in the big show when I never was really in a big city before. But I guess I seen enough of life not to be scared of the high buildings eh Al?

I will just give them what I got and if they don't like it they can send me back to the old Central and I will be perfectly satisfied.

I didn't know anybody was looking me over, but one of the boys told me that Jack Doyle the White Sox scout was down here looking at me when Grand Rapids was here. I beat them twice in that serious. You know Grand Rapids never had a chance with me when I was right. I shut them out in the first game and they got one run in the second on account of Flynn misjuging that fly ball. Anyway Doyle liked my work and he wired Comiskey to buy me. Comiskey come back with an offer and they excepted it. I don't know how much they got but anyway I am sold to the big league and believe me Al I will make good.

Well Al I will be home in a few days and we will have some of the good old times. Regards to all the boys and tell them I am still their pal and not all swelled up over this big league business.   Your pal,   JACK.

Chicago, Illinois, December 14.

OLD PAL: Well Al I have not got much to tell you. As you know Comiskey wrote me that if I was up in Chi this month to drop in and see him. So I got here Thursday morning and went to his office in the afternoon. His office is out to the ball park and believe me its some park and some office.

I went in and asked for Comiskey and a young fellow says He is not here now but can I do anything for you? I told him who I am and says I had an engagement to see Comiskey. He says The boss is out of town hunting and did I have to see him personally?

I says I wanted to see about signing a contract.

He told me I could sign as well with him as Comiskey and he took me into another office. He says What salary did you think you ought to get? and I says I wouldn't think of playing ball in the big league for less than three thousand dollars per annum. He laughed and says You don't want much. You better stick round town till the boss comes back. So here I am and it is costing me a dollar a day to stay at the hotel on Cottage Grove Avenue and that don't include my meals.

I generally eat at some of the cafes round the hotel but I had supper downtown last night and it cost me fifty-five cents. If Comiskey don't come back soon I won't have no more money left.

Speaking of money I won't sign no contract unless I get the salary you and I talked of, three thousand dollars. You know what I was getting in Terre Haute, a hundred and fifty a month, and I know it's going to cost me a lot more to live here. I made inquiries round here and find I can get board and room for eight dollars a week but I will be out of town half the time and will have to pay for my room when I am away or look up a new one when I come back. Then I will have to buy cloths to wear on the road in places like New York. When Comiskey comes back I will name him three thousand dollars as my lowest figure and I guess he will come through when he sees I am in ernest. I heard that Walsh was getting twice as much as that.

The papers says Comiskey will be back here sometime to-morrow. He has been hunting with the president of the league so he ought to feel pretty good. But I don't care how he feels. I am going to get a contract for three thousand and if he don't want to give it to me he can do the other thing. You know me Al.

Yours truly,   JACK.

Chicago, Illinois, December 16.

DEAR FRIEND AL: Well I will be home in a couple of days now but I wanted to write you and let you know how I come out with Comiskey. I signed my contract yesterday afternoon. He is a great old fellow Al and no wonder everybody likes him. He says Young man will you have a drink? But I was to smart and wouldn't take nothing. He says You was with Terre Haute? I says Yes I was. He says Doyle tells me you were pretty wild. I says Oh no I got good control. He says Well do you want to sign? I says Yes if I get my figure. He asks What is my figure and I says three thousand dollars per annum. He says Don't you want the office furniture too? Then he says I thought you was a young ball-player and I didn't know you wanted to buy my park.

We kidded each other back and forth like that a while and then he says You better go out and get the air and come back when you feel better. I says I feel O. K. now and I want to sign a contract because I have got to get back to Bedford. Then he calls the secretary and tells him to make out my contract. He give it to me and it calls for two hundred and fifty a month. He says You know we always have a city serious here in the fall where a fellow picks up a good bunch of money. I hadn't thought of that so I signed up. My yearly salary will be fifteen hundred dollars besides what the city serious brings me. And that is only for the first year. I will demand three thousand or four thousand dollars next year.

I would of started home on the evening train but I ordered a suit of cloths from a tailor over on Cottage Grove and it won't be done till tomorrow. It's going to cost me twenty bucks but it ought to last a long time. Regards to Frank and the bunch.   Your Pal,   JACK.

Paso Robles, California, March 2.

OLD PAL AL: Well Al we been in this little
berg now a couple of days and its bright and
warm all the time just like June. Seems funny
to have it so warm this early in March but I guess
this California climate is all they said about it
and then some.

It would take me a week to tell you about our
trip out here. We came on a Special Train De
Lukes and it was some train. Every place we
stopped there was crowds down to the station to
see us go through and all the people looked me
over like I was a actor or something. I guess
my hight and shoulders attracted their attention.
Well Al we finally got to Oakland which is across
part of the ocean from Frisco. We will be back
there later on for practice games.

We stayed in Oakland a few hours and then
took a train for here. It was another night in a
sleeper and believe me I was tired of sleepers before we got here. I have road one night at a
time but this was four straight nights. You know
Al I am not built right for a sleeping car birth.

The hotel here is a great big place and got good
eats. We got in at breakfast time and I made a
B line for the dining room. Kid Gleason who is
a kind of asst. manager to Callahan come in and

sat down with me. He says Leave something for the rest of the boys because they will be just as hungry as you. He says Ain't you afraid you will cut your throat with that knife. He says There ain't no extra charge for using the forks. He says You shouldn't ought to eat so much because you're overweight now. I says You may think I am fat, but it's all solid bone and muscle. He says Yes I suppose it's all solid bone from the neck up. I guess he thought I would get sore but I will let them kid me now because they will take off their hats to me when they see me work.

Manager Callahan called us all to his room after breakfast and give us a lecture. He says there would be no work for us the first day but that we must all take a long walk over the hills. He also says we must not take the training trip as a joke. Then the colored trainer give us our suits and I went to my room and tried mine on. I ain't a bad looking guy in the White Sox uniform Al. I will have my picture taken and send you boys some.

My roommate is Allen a lefthander from the Coast League. He don't look nothing like a pitcher but you can't never tell about them dam left handers. Well I didn't go on the long walk because I was tired out. Walsh stayed at the

hotel too and when he seen me he says Why didn't
you go with the bunch? I says I was too tired.
He says Well when Callahan comes back you better keep out of sight or tell him you are sick. I
says I don't care nothing for Callahan. He says
No but Callahan is crazy about you. He says
You better obey orders and you will git along
better. I guess Walsh thinks I am some rube.

When the bunch come back Callahan never
said a word to me but Gleason come up and says
Where was you? I told him I was too tired to
go walking. He says Well I will borrow a wheel-
barrow some place and push you round. He says
Do you sit down when you pitch? I let him kid
me because he has not saw my stuff yet.

Next morning half the bunch mostly vetrans
went to the ball park which isn't no better than
the one we got at home. Most of them was vetrans
as I say but I was in the bunch. That makes
things look pretty good for me don't it Al? We
tossed the ball round and hit fungos and run
round and then Callahan asks Scott and Russell
and I to warm up easy and pitch a few to the
batters. It was warm and I felt pretty good so
I warmed up pretty good. Scott pitched to them
first and kept laying them right over with noth-

ing on them. I don't believe a man gets any batting practice that way. So I went in and after
I lobbed a few over I cut loose my fast one. Lord
was to bat and he ducked out of the way and
then throwed his bat to the bench. Callahan says
What's the matter Harry? Lord says I forgot
to pay up my life insurance. He says I ain't
ready for Walter Johnson's July stuff.

Well Al I will make them think I am Walter
Johnson before I get through with them. But
Callahan come out to me and says What are you
trying to do kill somebody? He says Save your
smoke because you're going to need it later on.
He says Go easy with the boys at first or I won't
have no batters. But he was laughing and I
guess he was pleased to see the stuff I had.

There is a dance in the hotel to-night and I
am up in my room writing this in my underwear
while I get my suit pressed. I got it all mussed
up coming out here. I don't know what shoes
to wear. I asked Gleason and he says Wear your
baseball shoes and if any of the girls gets fresh
with you spike them. I guess he was kidding me.

Write and tell me all the news about home.

Yours truly,   JACK.

Paso Robles, California, March 7.

FRIEND AL: I showed them something out
there to-day Al. We had a game between two
teams. One team was made up of most of the
regulars and the other was made up of recruts.
I pitched three innings for the recruts and shut
the old birds out. I held them to one hit and
that was a ground ball that the recrut shortstop
Johnson ought to of ate up. I struck Collins out
and he is one of the best batters in the bunch.
I used my fast ball most of the while but showed
them a few spitters and they missed them a foot.
I guess I must of got Walsh's goat with my spitter because him and I walked back to the hotel
together and he talked like he was kind of jealous.
He says You will have to learn to cover up your
spitter. He says I could stand a mile away and
tell when you was going to throw it. He says
Some of these days I will learn you how to cover
it up. I guess Al I know how to cover it up all
right without Walsh learning me.

I always sit at the same table in the dining room
along with Gleason and Collins and Bodie and
Fournier and Allen the young lefthander I told
you about. I feel sorry for him because he never
says a word. To-night at supper Bodie says How
did I look to-day Kid? Gleason says Just like

you always do in the spring. You looked like a cow. Gleason seems to have the whole bunch scared of him and they let him say anything he wants to. I let him kid me to but I ain't scared of him. Collins then says to me You got some fast ball there boy. I says I was not as fast to-day as I am when I am right. He says Well then I don't want to hit against you when you are right. Then Gleason says to Collins Cut that stuff out. Then he says to me Don't believe what he tells you boy. If the pitchers in this league weren't no faster than you I would still be play-ing ball and I would be the best hitter in the country.

After supper Gleason went out on the porch with me. He says Boy you have got a little stuff but you have got a lot to learn. He says You field your position like a wash woman and you don't hold the runners up. He says When Chase was on second base to-day he got such a lead on you that the little catcher couldn't of shot him out at third with a rifle. I says They all thought I fielded my position all right in the Central League. He says Well if you think you do it all right you better go back to the Central League where you are appresiated. I says You can't send me back there because you could not get waivers.

He says Who would claim you? I says St. Louis and Boston and New York.

You know Al what Smith told me this winter. Gleason says Well if you're not willing to learn St. Louis and Boston and New York can have you and the first time you pitch against us we will steal fifty bases. Then he quit kidding and asked me to go to the field with him early to-morrow morning and he would learn me some things. I don't think he can learn me nothing but I promised I would go with him.

There is a little blonde kid in the hotel here who took a shine to me at the dance the other night but I am going to leave the skirts alone. She is real society and a swell dresser and she wants my picture. Regards to all the boys.

Your friend,   JACK.

P. S. The boys thought they would be smart to-night and put something over on me. A boy brought me a telegram and I opened it and it said You are sold to Jackson in the Cotton States League. For just a minute they had me going but then I happened to think that Jackson is in Michigan and there's no Cotton States League round there.

Paso Robles, California, March 9.

DEAR FRIEND AL: You have no doubt
read the good news in the papers before this
reaches you. I have been picked to go to Frisco
with the first team. We play practice games up
there about two weeks while the second club plays
in Los Angeles. Poor Allen had to go with the
second club. There's two other recrut pitchers
with our part of the team but my name was first
on the list so it looks like I had made good. I
knowed they would like my stuff when they seen
it. We leave here to-night. You got the first
team's address so you will know where to send
my mail. Callahan goes with us and Gleason
goes with the second club. Him and I have got
to be pretty good pals and I wish he was going
with us even if he don't let me eat like I want to.
He told me this morning to remember all he had
learned me and to keep working hard. He didn't
learn me nothing I didn't know before but I let
him think so.

The little blonde don't like to see me leave
here. She lives in Detroit and I may see her when
I go there. She wants me to write but I guess I
better not give her no encouragement.

Well Al I will write you a long letter from
Frisco.   Yours truly,   JACK.

Oakland, California, March 19.

DEAR OLD PAL: They have gave me plenty of work here all right. I have pitched four times but have not went over five innings yet. I worked against Oakland two times and against Frisco two times and only three runs have been scored off me. They should only ought to of had one but Bodie misjuged a easy fly ball in Frisco and Weaver made a wild peg in Oakland that let in a run. I am not using much but my fast ball but I have got a world of speed and they can't foul me when I am right. I whiffed eight men in five innings in Frisco yesterday and could of did better than that if I had of cut loose.

Manager Callahan is a funny guy and I don't understand him sometimes. I can't figure out if he is kidding or in ernest. We road back to Oakland on the ferry together after yesterday's game and he says Don't you never throw a slow ball? I says I don't need no slow ball with my spitter and my fast one. He says No of course you don't need it but if I was you I would get one of the boys to learn it to me. He says And you better watch the way the boys fields their positions and holds up the runners. He says To see you work a man might think they had a rule in the Central

League forbidding a pitcher from leaving the box or looking toward first base.

I told him the Central didn't have no rule like that. He says And I noticed you taking your wind up when What's His Name was on second base there to-day. I says Yes I got more stuff when I wind up. He says Of course you have but if you wind up like that with Cobb on base he will steal your watch and chain. I says Maybe Cobb can't get on base when I work against him. He says That's right and maybe San Francisco Bay is made of grapejuice. Then he walks away from me.

He give one of the youngsters a awful bawling out for something he done in the game at supper last night. If he ever talks to me like he done to him I will take a punch at him. You know me Al.

I come over to Frisco last night with some of the boys and we took in the sights. Frisco is some live town Al. We went all through China Town and the Barbers' Coast. Seen lots of swell dames but they was all painted up. They have beer out here that they call steam beer. I had a few glasses of it and it made me logey. A glass of that Terre Haute beer would go pretty good right now.

We leave here for Los Angeles in a few days and I will write you from there. This is some country Al and I would love to play ball round here.   Your Pal,   JACK.

P. S.—I got a letter from the little blonde and I suppose I got to answer it.

Los Angeles, California, March 26.

FRIEND AL: Only four more days of sunny California and then we start back East. We got exhibition games in Yuma and El Paso, Texas, and Oklahoma City and then we stop over in St. Joe, Missouri, for three days before we go home. You know Al we open the season in Cleveland and we won't be in Chi no more than just passing through. We don't play there till April eighteenth and I guess I will work in that serious all right against Detroit. Then I will be glad to have you and the boys come up and watch me as you suggested in your last letter.

I got another letter from the little blonde. She has went back to Detroit but she give me her address and telephone number and believe me Al I am going to look her up when we get there the twenty-ninth of April.

She is a stenographer and was out here with her uncle and aunt.

I had a run in with Kelly last night and it looked like I would have to take a wallop at him but the other boys seperated us. He is a bush outfielder from the New England League. We was playing poker. You know the boys plays poker a good deal but this was the first time I got in. I was having pretty good luck and was about four bucks to the good and I was thinking of quitting because I was tired and sleepy. Then Kelly opened the pot for fifty cents and I stayed. I had three sevens. No one else stayed. Kelly stood pat and I drawed two cards. And I catched my fourth seven. He bet fifty cents but I felt pretty safe even if he did have a pat hand. So I called him. I took the money and told them I was through.

Lord and some of the boys laughed but Kelly got nasty and begun to pan me for quitting and for the way I played. I says Well I won the pot didn't I? He says Yes and he called me something. I says I got a notion to take a punch at you.

He says Oh you have have you? And I come back at him. I says Yes I have have I? I would of busted his jaw if they hadn't stopped me. You know me Al.

I worked here two times once against Los Angeles and once against Venice. I went the full nine innings both times and Venice beat me four to two. I could of beat them easy with any kind of support. I walked a couple of guys in the forth and Chase drops a throw and Collins lets a fly ball get away from him. At that I would of shut them out if I had wanted to cut loose. After the game Callahan says You didn't look so good in there to-day. I says I didn't cut loose. He says Well you been working pretty near three weeks now and you ought to be in shape to cut loose. I says Oh I am in shape all right. He says Well don't work no harder than you have to or you might get hurt and then the league would blow up. I don't know if he was kidding me or not but I guess he thinks pretty well of me because he works me lots oftener than Walsh or Scott or Benz.

I will try to write you from Yuma, Texas, but we don't stay there only a day and I may not have time for a long letter.

Yours truly,   JACK.

Yuma, Arizona, April 1.

DEAR OLD AL: Just a line to let you know we are on our way back East. This place is in Arizona and it sure is sandy. They haven't got no regular ball club here and we play a pick-up team this afternoon. Callahan told me I would have to work. He says I am using you because we want to get through early and I know you can beat them quick. That is the first time he has said anything like that and I guess he is wiseing up that I got the goods.

We was talking about the Athaletics this morning and Callahan says None of you fellows pitch right to Baker. I was talking to Lord and Scott afterward and I say to Scott How do you pitch to Baker? He says I use my fadeaway. I says How do you throw it? He says Just like you throw a fast ball to anybody else. I says Why do you call it a fadeaway then? He says Because when I throw it to Baker it fades away over the fence.

This place is full of Indians and I wish you could see them Al. They don't look nothing like the Indians we seen in that show last summer.

Your old pal,   Jack.

Oklahoma City, April 4.

Friend Al: Coming out of Amarillo last night I and Lord and Weaver was sitting at a table in the dining car with a old lady. None of us were talking to her but she looked me over

pretty careful and seemed to kind of like my
looks. Finally she says Are you boys with some
football club? Lord nor Weaver didn't say nothing so I thought it was up to me and I says No
mam this is the Chicago White Sox Ball Club.
She says I knew you were athaletes. I says Yes
I guess you could spot us for athaletes. She says
Yes indeed and specially you. You certainly look
healthy. I says You ought to see me stripped.
I didn't see nothing funny about that but I
thought Lord and Weaver would die laughing.
Lord had to get up and leave the table and he
told everybody what I said.

All the boys wanted me to play poker on the
way here but I told them I didn't feel good. I
know enough to quit when I am ahead Al. Callahan and I sat down to breakfast all alone this
morning. He says Boy why don't you get to
work? I says What do you mean? Ain't I
working? He says You ain't improving none.
You have got the stuff to make a good pitcher
but you don't go after bunts and you don't cover
first base and you don't watch the baserunners.
He made me kind of sore talking that way and I
says Oh I guess I can get along all right.

He says Well I am going to put it up to you.
I am going to start you over in St. Joe day after

to-morrow and I want you to show me something.
I want you to cut loose with all you've got and
I want you to get round the infield a little and
show them you aren't tied in that box. I says Oh
I can field my position if I want to. He says
Well you better want to or I will have to ship
you back to the sticks. Then he got up and left.
He didn't scare me none Al. They won't ship
me to no sticks after the way I showed on this
trip and even if they did they couldn't get no
waivers on me.

Some of the boys have begun to call me Four
Sevens but it don't bother me none.

Yours truly,   JACK.

St. Joe, Missouri, April 7.

FRIEND AL: It rained yesterday so I worked
to-day instead and St. Joe done well to get three
hits. They couldn't of scored if we had played
all week. I give a couple of passes but I catched
a guy flatfooted off of first base and I come up
with a couple of bunts and throwed guys out.
When the game was over Callahan says That's
the way I like to see you work. You looked better to-day than you looked on the whole trip.
Just once you wound up with a man on but otherwise you was all O. K. So I guess my job is

cinched Al and I won't have to go to New York or St. Louis. I would rather be in Chi anyway because it is near home. I wouldn't care though if they traded me to Detroit. I hear from Violet right along and she says she can't hardly wait till I come to Detroit. She says she is strong for the Tigers but she will pull for me when I work against them. She is nuts over me and I guess she has saw lots of guys to.

I sent her a stickpin from Oklahoma City but I can't spend no more dough on her till after our first payday the fifteenth of the month. I had thirty bucks on me when I left home and I only got about ten left including the five spot I won in the poker game. I have to tip the waiters about thirty cents a day and I seen about twenty picture shows on the coast besides getting my cloths pressed a couple of times.

We leave here to-morrow night and arrive in Chi the next morning. The second club joins us there and then that night we go to Cleveland to open up. I asked one of the reporters if he knowed who was going to pitch the opening game and he says it would be Scott or Walsh but I guess he don't know much about it.

These reporters travel all round the country with the team all season and send in telegrams about the game every night. I ain't seen no Chi papers so I don't know what they been saying about me. But I should worry eh Al? Some of them are pretty nice fellows and some of them got the swell head. They hang round with the old fellows and play poker most of the time.

Will write you from Cleveland. You will see in the paper if I pitch the opening game.

Your old pal,   Jack.

Cleveland, Ohio, April 10.

Old Friend Al: Well Al we are all set to open the season this afternoon. I have just ate breakfast and I am sitting in the lobby of the hotel. I eat at a little lunch counter about a block from here and I saved seventy cents on breakfast. You see Al they give us a dollar a meal and if we don't want to spend that much all right. Our rooms at the hotel are paid for.

The Cleveland papers says Walsh or Scott will work for us this afternoon. I asked Callahan if there was any chance of me getting into the first game and he says I hope not. I don't know what he meant but he may surprise these reporters and let me pitch. I will beat them Al. Lajoie and Jackson is supposed to be great batters but the bigger they are the harder they fall.

The second team joined us yesterday in Chi and we practiced a little. Poor Allen was left in Chi last night with four others of the recruit pitchers. Looks pretty good for me eh Al? I only seen Gleason for a few minutes on the train last night. He says, Well you ain't took off much weight. You're hog fat. I says Oh I ain't fat. I didn't need to take off no weight. He says One good thing about it the club don't have to engage no birth for you because you spend all your time in the dining car. We kidded along like that a while and then the trainer rubbed my arm and I went to bed. Well Al I just got time to have my suit pressed before noon.

Yours truly,   JACK.

Cleveland, Ohio, April 11.

FRIEND AL: Well Al I suppose you know by this time that I did not pitch and that we got licked. Scott was in there and he didn't have nothing. When they had us beat four to one in the eight inning Callahan told me to go out and warm up and he put a batter in for Scott in our ninth. But Cleveland didn't have to play their ninth so I got no chance to work. But it looks like he means to start me in one of the games here. We got three more to play. Maybe I will pitch this afternoon. I got a postcard from Violet. She says Beat them Naps. I will give them a battle Al if I get a chance.

Glad to hear you boys have fixed it up to come to Chi during the Detroit serious. I will ask Callahan when he is going to pitch me and let you know. Thanks Al for the papers.

Your friend,   JACK.

St. Louis, Missouri, April 15.

FRIEND AL: Well Al I guess I showed them. I only worked one inning but I guess them Browns is glad I wasn't in there no longer than that. They had us beat seven to one in the sixth and Callahan pulls Benz out. I honestly felt sorry for him but he didn't have nothing, not a thing. They was hitting him so hard I thought they would score a hundred runs. A righthander name Bumgardner was pitching for them and he didn't look to have nothing either but we ain't got much of a batting team Al. I could hit better than some of them regulars. Anyway Callahan called Benz to the bench and sent for me. I was down in the corner warming up with Kuhn. I wasn't warmed up good but you know I got the nerve Al and I run right out there like I meant business. There was a man on second and nobody out when I come in. I didn't know who was up there but I found out afterward it was Shotten. He's the center-fielder. I was cold and I walked him. Then I got warmed up good and I made Johnston look like a boob. I give him three fast balls and he let two of them go by and missed the other one. I would of handed him a spitter but Schalk kept signing for fast ones and he knows more about them batters than me. Anyway I whiffed John-ston. Then up come Williams and I tried to make him hit at a couple of bad ones. I was in the hole with two balls and nothing and come right across the heart with my fast one. I wish you could of saw the hop on it. Williams hit it right straight up and Lord was camped under it. Then up come Pratt the best hitter on their club. You know what I done to him don't you Al? I give him one spitter and another he didn't strike at that was a ball. Then I come back with two fast ones and Mister Pratt was a dead baby. And you notice they didn't steal no bases neither.

In our half of the seventh inning Weaver and Schalk got on and I was going up there with a stick when Callahan calls me back and sends East-erly up. I don't know what kind of managing you call that. I hit good on the training trip and he must of knew they had no chance to score

off me in the innings they had left while they were
liable to murder his other pitchers. I come back
to the bench pretty hot and I says You're making
a mistake. He says If Comiskey had wanted you
to manage this team he would of hired you.

Then Easterly pops out and I says Now I
guess you're sorry you didn't let me hit. That
sent him right up in the air and he bawled me
awful. Honest Al I would of cracked him right
in the jaw if we hadn't been right out where
everybody could of saw us. Well he sent Cicotte
in to finish and they didn't score no more and
we didn't neither.

I road down in the car with Gleason. He says
Boy you shouldn't ought to talk like that to Cal.
Some day he will lose his temper and bust you
one. I says He won't never bust me. I says He
didn't have no right to talk like that to me. Gleason says I suppose you think he's going to laugh
and smile when we lost four out of the first five
games. He says Wait till to-night and then go
up to him and let him know you are sorry you
sassed him. I says I didn't sass him and I ain't
sorry.

So after supper I seen Callahan sitting in the
lobby and I went over and sit down by him. I
says When are you going to let me work? He

says I wouldn't never let you work only my pitchers are all shot to pieces. Then I told him about you boys coming up from Bedford to watch me during the Detroit serious and he says Well I will start you in the second game against Detroit. He says But I wouldn't if I had any pitchers. He says A girl could get out there and pitch better than some of them have been doing.

So you see Al I am going to pitch on the nineteenth. I hope you guys can be up there and I will show you something. I know I can beat them Tigers and I will have to do it even if they are Violet's team.

I notice that New York and Boston got trimmed to-day so I suppose they wish Comiskey would ask for waivers on me. No chance Al.

Your old pal,   JACK.

P. S.—We play eleven games in Chi and then go to Detroit. So I will see the little girl on the twenty-ninth.

Oh you Violet.

Chicago, Illinois, April 19.

DEAR OLD PAL: Well Al it's just as well you couldn't come. They beat me and I am writing you this so as you will know the truth about the game and not get a bum steer from what you read in the papers.

I had a sore arm when I was warming up and Callahan should never ought to of sent me in there. And Schalk kept signing for my fast ball and I kept giving it to him because I thought he ought to know something about the batters. Weaver and Lord and all of them kept kicking them round the infield and Collins and Bodie couldn't catch nothing.

Callahan ought never to of left me in there when he seen how sore my arm was. Why, I couldn't of threw hard enough to break a pain of glass my arm was so sore.

They sure did run wild on the bases. Cobb stole four and Bush and Crawford and Veach about two apiece. Schalk didn't even make a peg half the time. I guess he was trying to throw me down.

The score was sixteen to two when Callahan finally took me out in the eighth and I don't know how many more they got. I kept telling him to take me out when I seen how bad I was but he wouldn't do it. They started bunting in the fifth and Lord and Chase just stood there and didn't give me no help at all.

I was all O. K. till I had the first two men out

in the first inning. Then Crawford come up. I
wanted to give him a spitter but Schalk signs me
for the fast one and I give it to him. The ball
didn't hop much and Crawford happened to catch
it just right. At that Collins ought to of catched
the ball. Crawford made three bases and up
come Cobb. It was the first time I ever seen him.
He hollered at me right off the reel. He says
You better walk me you busher. I says I will
walk you back to the bench. Schalk signs for a
spitter and I gives it to him and Cobb misses it.

Then instead of signing for another one Schalk
asks for a fast one and I shook my head no but
he signed for it again and yells Put something
on it. So I throwed a fast one and Cobb hits it
right over second base. I don't know what
Weaver was doing but he never made a move for
the ball. Crawford scored and Cobb was on first
base. First thing I knowed he had stole second
while I held the ball. Callahan yells Wake up
out there and I says Why don't your catcher tell
me when they are going to steal. Schalk says
Get in there and pitch and shut your mouth. Then
I got mad and walked Veach and Moriarty but
before I walked Moriarty Cobb and Veach pulled
a double steal on Schalk. Gainor lifts a fly and

Lord drops it and two more come in. Then Stanage walks and I whiffs their pitcher.

I come in to the bench and Callahan says Are your friends from Bedford up here? I was pretty sore and I says Why don't you get a catcher? He says We don't need no catcher when you're pitching because you can't get nothing past their bats. Then he says You better leave your uniform in here when you go out next inning or Cobb will steal it off your back. I says My arm is sore. He says Use your other one and you'll do just as good.

Gleason says Who do you want to warm up? Callahan says Nobody. He says Cobb is going to lead the league in batting and basestealing anyway so we might as well give him a good start. I was mad enough to punch his jaw but the boys winked at me not to do nothing.

Well I got some support in the next inning and nobody got on. Between innings I says Well I guess I look better now don't I? Callahan says Yes but you wouldn't look so good if Collins hadn't jumped up on the fence and catched that one off Crawford. That's all the encouragement I got Al.

Cobb come up again to start the third and when Schalk signs me for a fast one I shakes my head.

Then Schalk says All right pitch anything you want to. I pitched a spitter and Cobb bunts it right at me. I would of threw him out a block but I stubbed my toe in a rough place and fell down. This is the roughest ground I ever seen Al. Veach bunts and for a wonder Lord throws him out. Cobb goes to second and honest Al I forgot all about him being there and first thing I knowed he had stole third. Then Moriarty hits a fly ball to Bodie and Cobb scores though Bodie ought to of threw him out twenty feet.

They batted all round in the forth inning and scored four or five more. Crawford got the luckiest three-base hit I ever see. He popped one way up in the air and the wind blowed it against the fence. The wind is something fierce here Al. At that Collins ought to of got under it.

I was looking at the bench all the time expecting Callahan to call me in but he kept hollering Go on and pitch. Your friends wants to see you pitch.

Well Al I don't know how they got the rest of their runs but they had more luck than any team I ever seen. And all the time Jennings was on the coaching line yelling like a Indian. Some day Al I'm going to punch his jaw.

After Veach had hit one in the eight Callahan

calls me to the bench and says You're through for the day. I says It's about time you found out my arm was sore. He says I ain't worrying about your arm but I'm afraid some of our outfielders will run their legs off and some of them poor infielders will get killed. He says The reporters just sent me a message saying they had run out of paper. Then he says I wish some of the other clubs had pitchers like you so we could hit once in a while. He says Go in the clubhouse and get your arm rubbed off. That's the only way I can get Jennings sore he says.

Well Al that's about all there was to it. It will take two or three stamps to send this but I want you to know the truth about it. The way my arm was I ought never to of went in there.

Yours truly,   JACK.

Chicago, Illinois, April 25.

FRIEND AL: Just a line to let you know I am still on earth. My arm feels pretty good again and I guess maybe I will work at Detroit. Violet writes that she can't hardly wait to see me. Looks like I got a regular girl now Al. We go up there the twenty-ninth and maybe I won't be glad to see her. I hope she will be out to the game the day I pitch. I will pitch the way I want to next time and them Tigers won't have such a picnic.

I suppose you seen what the Chicago reporters said about that game. I will punch a couple.of their jaws when I see them.

Your pal,   JACK.

Chicago, Illinois, April 29.

DEAR OLD AL: Well Al it's all over. The club went to Detroit last night and I didn't go along. Callahan told me to report to Comiskey this morning and I went up to the office at ten o'clock. He give me my pay to date and broke the news. I am sold to Frisco.

I asked him how they got waivers on me and he says Oh there was no trouble about that because they all heard how you tamed the Tigers. Then he patted me on the back and says Go out there and work hard boy and maybe you'll get another chance some day. I was kind of choked up so I walked out of the office.

I ain't had no fair deal Al and I ain't going to no Frisco. I will quit the game first and take that job Charley offered me at the billiard hall.

I expect to be in Bedford in a couple of days. I have got to pack up first and settle with my landlady about my room here which I engaged for all season thinking I would be treated square. I am going to rest and lay round home a while and try to forget this rotten game. Tell the boys about it Al and tell them I never would of got let out if I hadn't worked with a sore arm.

I feel sorry for that little girl up in Detroit Al. She expected me there today.

Your old pal,   JACK.

P. S. I suppose you seen where that lucky lefthander Allen shut out Cleveland with two hits yesterday. The lucky stiff.

2

The Busher Comes Back

San Francisco, California, May 13.

FRIEND AL: I suppose you and the rest of the boys in Bedford will be supprised to learn that I am out here, because I remember telling you when I was sold to San Francisco by the White Sox that not under no circumstances would I report here. I was pretty mad when Comiskey give me my release, because I didn't think I had been given a fair show by Callahan. I don't think so yet Al and I never will but Bill Sullivan the old White Sox catcher talked to me and told me not to pull no boner by refuseing to go where they sent me. He says You're only hurting yourself. He says You must remember that this was your first time up in the big show and very few men no matter how much stuff they got can expect to make good right off the reel. He says All you need is experience and pitching out in the Coast League will be just the thing for you.

So I went in and asked Comiskey for my transportation and he says That's right Boy go out there and work hard and maybe I will want you back. I told him I hoped so but I don't hope nothing of the kind Al. I am going to see if I can't get Detroit to buy me, because I would rather live in Detroit than anywheres else. The little girl who got stuck on me this spring lives there. I guess I told you about her Al. Her name is Violet and she is some queen. And then if I got with the Tigers I wouldn't never have to pitch against Cobb and Crawford, though I believe I could show both of them up if I was right. They ain't got much of a ball club here and hardly any good pitchers outside of me. But I don't care.

I will win some games if they give me any support and I will get back in the big league and show them birds something. You know me, Al.

Your pal,   JACK.

Los Angeles, California, May 20.

AL: Well old pal I don't suppose you can find much news of this league in the papers at home so you may not know that I have been standing this league on their heads. I pitched against Oakland up home and shut them out with two hits. I made them look like suckers Al. They hadn't never saw no speed like mine and they was scared to death the minute I cut loose. I could of pitched the last six innings with my foot and trimmed them they was so scared.

Well we come down here for a serious and I worked the second game. They got four hits and one run, and I just give them the one run. Their shortstop Johnson was on the training trip with the White Sox and of course I knowed him pretty well. So I eased up in the last inning and let him hit one. If I had of wanted to let myself out he couldn't of hit me with a board. So I am going along good and Howard our manager says he is going to use me regular. He's a pretty nice manager and not a bit sarkastic like some of them big leaguers. I am fielding my position good and watching the baserunners to. Thank goodness Al they ain't no Cobbs in this league and a man ain't scared of haveing his uniform stole off his back.

But listen Al I don't want to be bought by Detroit no more. It is all off between Violet and I. She wasn't the sort of girl I suspected. She is just like them all Al. No heart. I wrote her a letter from Chicago telling her I was sold to San Francisco and she wrote back a postcard saying something about not haveing no time to waste on bushers. What do you know about that Al?

Calling me a busher. I will show them. She wasn't no good Al and I figure I am well rid of her. Good riddance is rubbish as they say.

I will let you know how I get along and if I hear anything about being sold or drafted.

Yours truly,   JACK.

San Francisco, California, July 20.

FRIEND AL: You will forgive me for not writeing to you oftener when you hear the news I got for you. Old pal I am engaged to be married. Her name is Hazel Carney and she is some queen, Al—a great big stropping girl that must weigh one hundred and sixty lbs. She is out to every game and she got stuck on me from watching me work.

Then she writes a note to me and makes a date and I meet her down on Market Street one night. We go to a nickel show together and have some time. Since then we been together pretty near every evening except when I was away on the road.

Night before last she asked me if I was married and I tells her No and she says a big handsome man like I ought not to have no trouble finding a wife. I tells her I ain't never looked for one and she says Well you wouldn't have to look very far. I asked her if she was married and she said No but she wouldn't mind it. She likes her beer pretty well and her and I had several and I guess I was feeling pretty good. Anyway I guess I asked her if she wouldn't marry me and she says it was O. K. I ain't a bit sorry Al because she is some doll and will make them all sit up back home. She wanted to get married right away but I said No wait till the season is over and maybe I will have more dough. She asked me what I was getting and I told her two hundred dollars a month. She says she didn't think I was getting enough and I don't neither but I will get the money when I get up in the big show again.

Anyway we are going to get married this fall and then I will bring her home and show her to you. She wants to live in Chi or New York but I guess she will like Bedford O. K. when she gets acquainted.

I have made good here all right Al. Up to a week ago Sunday I had won eleven straight. I have lost a couple since then, but one day I wasn't feeling good and the other time they kicked it away behind me.

I had a run in with Howard after Portland had beat me. He says Keep on running round with that skirt and you won't never win another game.

He says Go to bed nights and keep in shape or I will take your money. I told him to mind his own business and then he walked away from me. I guess he was scared I was going to smash him. No manager ain't going to bluff me Al.

So I went to bed early last night and didn't keep my date with the kid. She was pretty sore about it but business before plesure Al. Don't tell the boys nothing about me being engaged. I want to surprise them.   Your pal,   JACK.

Sacramento, California, August 16.

FRIEND AL: Well Al I got the supprise of my life last night. Howard called me up after I got to my room and tells me I am going back to the White Sox. Come to find out, when they sold me out here they kept a option on me and yesterday they exercised it. He told me I would have to report at once. So I packed up as quick as I could and then went down to say good-by to the kid. She was all broke up and wanted to go along with me but I told her I didn't have enough dough to get married. She said she would come anyway and we could get married in Chi but I told her she better wait. She cried all over my sleeve. She sure is gone on me Al and I couldn't help feeling sorry for her but I promised to send for her in October and then everything will be all O. K. She asked me how much I was going to get in the big league and I told her I would get a lot more money than out here because I wouldn't play if I didn't. You know me Al.

I come over here to Sacramento with the club this morning and I am leaveing to-night for Chi. I will get there next Tuesday and I guess Callahan will work me right away because he must of seen his mistake in letting me go by now. I will show them Al.

I looked up the skedule and I seen where we play in Detroit the fifth and sixth of September. I hope they will let me pitch there Al. Violet goes to the games and I will make her sorry she give me that kind of treatment. And I will make them Tigers sorry they kidded me last spring. I ain't afraid of Cobb or none of them now, Al.

Your pal,   JACK.

Chicago Illinois, August 27.

AL: Well old pal I guess I busted in right. Did you notice what I done to them Athaletics, the best ball club in the country? I bet Violet wishes she hadn't called me no busher.

I got here last Tuesday and set up in the stand and watched the game that afternoon. Washington was playing here and Johnson pitched. I was anxious to watch him because I had heard so much about him. Honest Al he ain't as fast as me. He shut them out, but they never was much of a hitting club. I went to the clubhouse after the game and shook hands with the bunch. Kid Gleason the assistant manager seemed pretty glad to see me and he says Well have you learned something? I says Yes I guess I have. He says Did you see the game this afternoon? I says I had and he asked me what I thought of Johnson. I says I don't think so much of him. He says Well I guess you ain't learned nothing then. He says What was the matter with Johnson's work? I says He ain't got nothing but a fast ball. Then he says Yes and Rockefeller ain't got nothing but a hundred million bucks.

Well I asked Callahan if he was going to give me a chance to work and he says he was. But I sat on the bench a couple of days and he didn't ask me to do nothing. Finally I asked him why not and he says I am saving you to work against a good club, the Athaletics. Well the Athaletics come and I guess you know by this time what I done to them. And I had to work against Bender at that but I ain't afraid of none of them now Al.

Baker didn't hit one hard all afternoon and I didn't have no trouble with Collins neither. I let them down with five blows all though the papers give them seven. Them reporters here don't no more about scoreing than some old woman. They give Barry a hit on a fly ball that Bodie ought to of eat up, only he stumbled or something and they handed Oldring a two base hit on a ball that Weaver had to duck to get out of the way from. But I don't care nothing about reporters. I beat them Athaletics and beat them good, five to one. Gleason slapped me on the back after the game and says Well you learned something after all. Rub some arnicky on your head to keep the swelling down and you may be a real pitcher yet. I says I ain't got no swell head. He says No. If I hated myself like you do I would be a moveing picture actor.

Well I asked Callahan would he let me pitch up to Detroit and he says Sure. He says Do you want to get revenge on them? I says, Yes I did. He says Well you have certainly got some comeing. He says I never seen no man get worse treatment than them Tigers give you last spring. I says Well they won't do it this time because I will

know how to pitch to them. He says How are
you going to pitch to Cobb? I says I am going
to feed him on my slow one. He says Well Cobb
had ought to make a good meal off of that. Then
we quit jokeing and he says You have improved
a hole lot and I am going to work you right along
regular and if you can stand the gaff I may be
able to use you in the city serious. You know Al
the White Sox plays a city serious every fall with
the Cubs and the players makes quite a lot of
money. The winners gets about eight hundred
dollars a peace and the losers about five hundred.
We will be the winners if I have anything to say
about it.

I am tickled to death at the chance of working
in Detroit and I can't hardly wait till we get
there. Watch my smoke Al.

Your pal,   JACK.

P. S. I am going over to Allen's flat to play
cards a while to-night. Allen is the left-hander
that was on the training trip with us. He ain't
got a thing, Al, and I don't see how he gets by.
He is married and his wife's sister is visiting them.
She wants to meet me but it won't do her much
good. I seen her out to the game today and she
ain't much for looks.

Detroit, Mich., September 6.

FRIEND AL: I got a hole lot to write but I ain't got much time because we are going over to Cleveland on the boat at ten P. M. I made them Tigers like it Al just like I said I would. And what do you think, Al, Violet called me up after the game and wanted to see me but I will tell you about the game first.

They got one hit off of me and Cobb made it a scratch single that he beat out. If he hadn't of been so dam fast I would of had a no hit game. At that Weaver could of threw him out if he had of started after the ball in time. Crawford didn't get nothing like a hit and I whiffed him once. I give two walks both of them to Bush but he is such a little guy that you can't pitch to him.

When I was warming up before the game Callahan was standing beside me and pretty soon Jennings come over. Jennings says You ain't going to pitch that bird are you? And Callahan said Yes he was. Then Jennings says I wish you wouldn't because my boys is all tired out and can't run the bases. Callahan says They won't get no chance to-day. No, says Jennings I suppose not. I suppose he will walk them all and they won't have to run. Callahan says He won't give no bases on balls, he says. But you better

tell your gang that he is liable to bean them and
they better stay away from the plate. Jennings
says He won't never hurt my boys by beaning
them. Then I cut in. Nor you neither, I says.
Callahan laughs at that so I guess I must of pulled
a pretty good one. Jennings didn't have no comeback so he walks away.

Then Cobb come over and asked if I was going
to work. Callahan told him Yes. Cobb says
How many innings? Callahan says All the way.
Then Cobb says Be a good fellow Cal and take
him out early. I am lame and can't run. I butts
in then and said Don't worry, Cobb. You won't
have to run because we have got a catcher who
can hold them third strikes. Callahan laughed
again and says to me You sure did learn something out on that Coast.

Well I walked Bush right off the real and they
all begun to holler on the Detroit bench There
he goes again. Vitt come up and Jennings yells
Leave your bat in the bag Osker. He can't get
them over. But I got them over for that bird all
O. K. and he pops out trying to bunt. And then
I whiffed Crawford. He starts off with a foul
that had me scared for a minute because it was
pretty close to the foul line and it went clear out
of the park. But he missed a spitter a foot and

then I supprised them Al. I give him a slow ball
and I honestly had to laugh to see him lunge for
it. I bet he must of strained himself. He throwed
his bat way like he was mad and I guess he
was. Cobb came pranceing up like he always does
and yells Give me that slow one Boy. So I says
All right. But I fooled him. Instead of giveing
him a slow one like I said I was going I handed
him a spitter. He hit it all right but it was a
line drive right in Chase's hands. He says Pretty
lucky Boy but I will get you next time. I come
right back at him. I says Yes you will.

Well Al I had them going like that all through.
About the sixth inning Callahan yells from the
bench to Jennings What do you think of him
now? And Jennings didn't say nothing. What
could he of said?

Cobb makes their one hit in the eighth. He
never would of made it if Schalk had of let me
throw him spitters instead of fast ones. At that
Weaver ought to of threw him out. Anyway they
didn't score and we made a monkey out of Du-
buque, or whatever his name is.

Well Al I got back to the hotel and snuck down
the street a ways and had a couple of beers before supper. So I come to the supper table late
and Walsh tells me they had been several phone

calls for me. I go down to the desk and they tell me to call up a certain number. So I called up and they charged me a nickel for it. A girl's voice answers the phone and I says Was they some one there that wanted to talk to Jack Keefe? She says You bet they is. She says Don't you know me, Jack? This is Violet. Well, you could of knocked me down with a peace of bread. I says What do you want? She says Why I want to see you. I says Well you can't see me. She says Why what's the matter, Jack? What have I did that you should be sore at me? I says I guess you know all right. You called me a busher. She says Why I didn't do nothing of the kind. I says Yes you did on that postcard. She says I didn't write you no postcard.

Then we argued along for a while and she swore up and down that she didn't write me no postcard or call me no busher. I says Well then why didn't you write me a letter when I was in Frisco? She says she had lost my address. Well Al I don't know if she was telling me the truth or not but may be she didn't write that postcard after all. She was crying over the telephone so I says Well it is too late for I and you to get together because I am engaged to be married. Then she screamed and I hang up the receiver. She

must of called back two or three times because
they was calling my name round the hotel but
I wouldn't go near the phone. You know me Al.

Well when I hang up and went back to finish
my supper the dining room was locked. So I had
to go out and buy myself a sandwich. They
soaked me fifteen cents for a sandwich and a cup
of coffee so with the nickel for the phone I am
out twenty cents altogether for nothing. But
then I would of had to tip the waiter in the hotel
a dime.

Well Al I must close and catch the boat. I
expect a letter from Hazel in Cleveland and
maybe Violet will write to me too. She is stuck
on me all right Al. I can see that. And I don't
believe she could of wrote that postcard after all.

Yours truly,   JACK.

Boston, Massachusetts, September 12.

OLD PAL: Well Al I got a letter from Hazel
in Cleveland and she is comeing to Chi in October for the city serious. She asked me to send
her a hundred dollars for her fare and to buy
some cloths with. I sent her thirty dollars for
the fare and told her she could wait till she got
to Chi to buy her cloths. She said she would give
me the money back as soon as she seen me but

she is a little short now because one of her girl friends borrowed fifty off of her. I guess she must be pretty soft-hearted Al. I hope you and Bertha can come up for the wedding because I would like to have you stand up with me.

I all so got a letter from Violet and they was blots all over it like she had been crying. She swore she did not write that postcard and said she would die if I didn't believe her. She wants to know who the lucky girl is who I am engaged to be married to. I believe her Al when she says she did not write that postcard but it is too late now. I will let you know the date of my wedding as soon as I find out.

I guess you seen what I done in Cleveland and here. Allen was going awful bad in Cleveland and I relieved him in the eighth when we had a lead of two runs. I put them out in one-two-three order in the eighth but had hard work in the ninth due to rotten support. I walked Johnston and Chapman and Turner sacrificed them ahead. Jackson come up then and I had two strikes on him. I could of whiffed him but Schalk makes me give him a fast one when I wanted to give him a slow one. He hit it to Berger and Johnston ought to of been threw out at the plate but Berger fumbles and then has to

make the play at first base. He got Jackson all
O. K. but they was only one run behind then
and Chapman was on third base. Lajoie was up
next and Callahan sends out word for me to walk
him. I thought that was rotten manageing because Lajoie or no one else can hit me when I
want to cut loose. So after I give him two bad
balls I tried to slip over a strike on him but the
lucky stiff hit it on a line to Weaver. Anyway
the game was over and I felt pretty good. But
Callahan don't appresiate good work Al. He give
me a call in the clubhouse and said if I ever dis-
obeyed his orders again he would suspend me
without no pay and lick me too. Honest Al it
was all I could do to keep from wrapping his jaw
but Gleason winks at me not to do nothing.

I worked the second game here and give them
three hits two of which was bunts that Lord
ought to of eat up. I got better support in Frisco
than I been getting here Al. But I don't care.
The Boston bunch couldn't of hit me with a shov-
vel and we beat them two to nothing. I worked
against Wood at that. They call him Smoky Joe
and they say he has got a lot of speed.

Boston is some town, Al, and I wish you and
Bertha could come here sometime. I went down
to the wharf this morning and seen them unload

the fish. They must of been a million of them but I didn't have time to count them. Every one of them was five or six times as big as a blue gill.

Violet asked me what would be my address in New York City so I am dropping her a postcard to let her know all though I don't know what good it will do her. I certainly won't start no correspondents with her now that I am engaged to be married. Yours truly, JACK.

New York, New York, September 16.

FRIEND AL: I opened the serious here and beat them easy but I know you must of saw about it in the Chi papers. At that they don't give me no fair show in the Chi papers. One of the boys bought one here and I seen in it where I was lucky to win that game in Cleveland. If I knowed which one of them reporters wrote that I would punch his jaw.

Al I told you Boston was some town but this is the real one. I never seen nothing like it and I been going some since we got here. I walked down Broadway the Main Street last night and I run into a couple of the ball players and they took me to what they call the Garden but it ain't like the gardens at home because this one is indoors. We sat down to a table and had several

drinks. Pretty soon one of the boys asked me
if I was broke and I says No, why? He says You
better get some lubricateing oil and loosen up. I
don't know what he meant but pretty soon when
we had had a lot of drinks the waiter brings a
check and hands it to me. It was for one dollar.
I says Oh I ain't paying for all of them. The
waiter says This is just for that last drink.

I thought the other boys would make a holler
but they didn't say nothing. So I give him a dollar bill and even then he didn't act satisfied so
I asked him what he was waiting for and he said
Oh nothing, kind of sassy. I was going to bust
him but the boys give me the sign to shut up and
not to say nothing. I excused myself pretty soon
because I wanted to get some air. I give my check
for my hat to a boy and he brought my hat and
I started going and he says Haven't you forgot
something? I guess he must of thought I was
wearing a overcoat.

Then I went down the Main Street again and
some man stopped me and asked me did I want
to go to the show. He said he had a ticket. I
asked him what show and he said the Follies. I
never heard of it but I told him I would go if he
had a ticket to spare. He says I will spare you
this one for three dollars. I says You must take

me for some boob. He says No I wouldn't insult no boob. So I walks on but if he had of insulted me I would of busted him.

I went back to the hotel then and run into Kid Gleason. He asked me to take a walk with him so out I go again. We went to the corner and he bought me a beer. He don't drink nothing but pop himself. The two drinks was only ten cents so I says This is the place for me. He says Where have you been? and I told him about paying one dollar for three drinks. He says I see I will have to take charge of you. Don't go round with them ball players no more. When you want to go out and see the sights come to me and I will stear you. So to-night he is going to stear me. I will write to you from Philadelphia.

Your pal,   JACK.

Philadelphia, Pa., September 19.

FRIEND AL: They won't be no game here to-day because it is raining. We all been loafing round the hotel all day and I am glad of it because I got all tired out over in New York City. I and Kid Gleason went round together the last couple of nights over there and he wouldn't let me spend no money. I seen a lot of girls that I would of liked to of got acquainted with but he wouldn't even let me answer them when they spoke to me. We run in to a couple of peaches last night and they had us spotted too. One of them says I'll bet you're a couple of ball players. But Kid says You lose your bet. I am a bellhop and the big rube with me is nothing but a pitcher.

One of them says What are you trying to do kid somebody? He says Go home and get some soap and remove your disguise from your face. I didn't think he ought to talk like that to them and I called him about it and said maybe they was lonesome and it wouldn't hurt none if we treated them to a soda or something. But he says Lonesome. If I don't get you away from here they will steal everything you got. They won't even leave you your fast ball. So we left them and he took me to a picture show. It was some California pictures and they made me think of Hazel so when I got back to the hotel I sent her three postcards.

Gleason made me go to my room at ten o'clock both nights but I was pretty tired anyway because he had walked me all over town. I guess we must of saw twenty shows. He says I would take you to the grand opera only it would be throwing money away because we can hear Ed

Walsh for nothing. Walsh has got some voice
Al a loud high tenor.

To-morrow is Sunday and we have a double
header Monday on account of the rain to-day.
I thought sure I would get another chance to beat
the Athaletics and I asked Callahan if he was
going to pitch me here but he said he thought he
would save me to work against Johnson in Washington. So you see Al he must figure I am about
the best he has got. I'll beat him Al if they get a
couple of runs behind me.

Yours truly,   JACK.

P. S.   They was a letter here from Violet and
it pretty near made me feel like crying. I wish
they was two of me so both them girls could be
happy.

Washington, D. C., September 22.

DEAR OLD AL: Well Al here I am in the
capital of the old United States. We got in last
night and I been walking round town all morning.
But I didn't tire myself out because I am going
to pitch against Johnson this afternoon.

This is the prettiest town I ever seen but I believe they is more colored people here than they
is in Evansville or Chi. I seen the White House
and the Monumunt. They say that Bill Sulli-

van and Gabby St. once catched a baseball that
was threw off of the top of the Monumunt but
I bet they couldn't catch it if I throwed it.

I was in to breakfast this morning with Gleason and Bodie and Weaver and Fournier. Gleason says I'm supprised that you ain't sick in bed
to-day. I says Why?

He says Most of our pitchers gets sick when
Cal tells them they are going to work against
Johnson. He says Here's these other fellows all
feeling pretty sick this morning and they ain't
even pitchers. All they have to do is hit against
him but it looks like as if Cal would have to send
substitutes in for them. Bodie is complaining of a
sore arm which he must of strained drawing to
two card flushes. Fournier and Weaver have
strained their legs doing the tango dance. Nothing could cure them except to hear that big Walter
had got throwed out of his machine and wouldn't
be able to pitch against us in this serious.

I says I feel O. K. and I ain't afraid to pitch
against Johnson and I ain't afraid to hit against
him neither. Then Weaver says Have you ever
saw him work? Yes, I says, I seen him in Chi.
Then Weaver says Well if you have saw him
work and ain't afraid to hit against him I'll bet
you would go down to Wall Street and holler

Hurrah for Roosevelt. I says No I wouldn't do that but I ain't afraid of no pitcher and what is more if you get me a couple of runs I'll beat him. Then Fournier says Oh we will get you a couple of runs all right. He says That's just as easy as catching whales with a angleworm.

Well Al I must close and go in and get some lunch. My arm feels great and they will have to go some to beat me Johnson or no Johnson.

Your pal,   JACK.

Washington, D. C., September 22.

FRIEND AL: Well I guess you know by this time that they didn't get no two runs for me, only one, but I beat him just the same. I beat him one to nothing and Callahan was so pleased that he give me a ticket to the theater. I just got back from there and it is pretty late and I already have wrote you one letter to-day but I am going to sit up and tell you about it.

It was cloudy before the game started and when I was warming up I made the remark to Callahan that the dark day ought to make my speed good. He says Yes and of course it will handicap John-son.

While Washington was takeing their practice their two coachers Schaefer and Altrock got out

on the infield and cut up and I pretty near busted
laughing at them. They certainly is funny Al.
Callahan asked me what was I laughing at and
I told him and he says That's the first time I
ever seen a pitcher laugh when he was going to
work against Johnson. He says Griffith is a
pretty good fellow to give us something to laugh
at before he shoots that guy at us.

I warmed up good and told Schalk not to ask
me for my spitter much because my fast one looked
faster than I ever seen it. He says it won't make
much difference what you pitch to-day. I says
Oh, yes, it will because Callahan thinks enough
of me to work me against Johnson and I want
to show him he didn't make no mistake. Then
Gleason says No he didn't make no mistake.
Wasteing Cicotte or Scotty would of been a mistake in this game.

Well, Johnson whiffs Weaver and Chase and
makes Lord pop out in the first inning. I walked
their first guy but I didn't give Milan nothing to
bunt and finally he flied out. And then I whiffed
the next two. On the bench Callahan says That's
the way, boy. Keep that up and we got a chance.

Johnson had fanned four of us when I come up
with two out in the third inning and he whiffed
me to. I fouled one though that if I had ever

got a good hold of I would of knocked out of the park. In the first seven innings we didn't have a hit off of him. They had got five or six lucky ones off of me and I had walked two or three, but I cut loose with all I had when they was men on and they couldn't do nothing with me. The only reason I walked so many was because my fast one was jumping so. Honest Al it was so fast that Evans the umpire couldn't see it half the time and he called a lot of balls that was right over the heart.

Well I come up in the eighth with two out and the score still nothing and nothing. I had whiffed the second time as well as the first but it was account of Evans missing one on me. The eighth started with Shanks muffing a fly ball off of Bodie. It was way out by the fence so he got two bases on it and he went to third while they was throwing Berger out. Then Schalk whiffed.

Callahan says Go up and try to meet one Jack. It might as well be you as anybody else. But your old pal didn't whiff this time Al. He gets two strikes on me with fast ones and then I passed up two bad ones. I took my healthy at the next one and slapped it over first base. I guess I could of made two bases on it but I didn't want to tire myself out. Anyway Bodie scored and I had them beat. And my hit was the only one we got off of him so I guess he is a pretty good pitcher after all Al.

They filled up the bases on me with one out in the ninth but it was pretty dark then and I made McBride and their catcher look like suckers with my speed.

I felt so good after the game that I drunk one of them pink cocktails. I don't know what their name is. And then I sent a postcard to poor little Violet. I don't care nothing about her but it don't hurt me none to try and cheer her up once in a while. We leave here Thursday night for home and they had ought to be two or three letters there for me from Hazel because I haven't heard from her lately. She must of lost my road addresses.

Your pal,   JACK.

P. S. I forgot to tell you what Callahan said after the game. He said I was a real pitcher now and he is going to use me in the city serious. If he does Al we will beat them Cubs sure.

Chicago, Illinois, September 27.

FRIEND AL: They wasn't no letter here at all from Hazel and I guess she must of been sick.

Or maybe she didn't think it was worth while writeing as long as she is comeing next week.

I want to ask you to do me a favor Al and that is to see if you can find me a house down there. I will want to move in with Mrs. Keefe, don't that sound funny Al? sometime in the week of October twelfth. Old man Cutting's house or that yellow house across from you would be O. K. I would rather have the yellow one so as to be near you. Find out how much rent they want Al and if it is not no more than twelve dollars a month get it for me. We will buy our furniture here in Chi when Hazel comes.

We have a couple of days off now Al and then we play St. Louis two games here. Then Detroit comes to finish the season the third and fourth of October.

Your pal,   Jack.

Chicago, Illinois, October 3.

Dear Old Al: Thanks Al for getting the house. The one-year lease is O. K. You and Bertha and me and Hazel can have all sorts of good times together. I guess the walk needs repairs but I can fix that up when I come. We can stay at the hotel when we first get there.

I wish you could of came up for the city serious Al but anyway I want you and Bertha to be sure and come up for our wedding. I will let you know the date as soon as Hazel gets here.

The serious starts Tuesday and this town is wild over it. The Cubs finished second in their league and we was fifth in ours but that don't scare me none. We would of finished right on top if I had of been here all season.

Callahan pitched one of the bushers against Detroit this afternoon and they beat him bad. Callahan is saveing up Scott and Allen and Russell and Cicotte and I for the big show. Walsh isn't in no shape and neither is Benz. It looks like I would have a good deal to do because most of them others can't work no more than once in four days and Allen ain't no good at all.

We have a day to rest after to-morrow's game with the Tigers and then we go at them Cubs.

Your pal, JACK.

P. S. I have got it figured that Hazel is fixing to surprise me by dropping in on me because I haven't heard nothing yet.

Chicago, Illinois, October 7.

FRIEND AL: Well Al you know by this time that they beat me to-day and tied up the serious. But I have still got plenty of time Al and I will get them before it is over. My arm wasn't feeling good Al and my fast ball didn't hop like it had ought to. But it was the rotten support I got that beat me. That lucky stiff Zimmerman was the only guy that got a real hit off of me and he must of shut his eyes and throwed his bat because the ball he hit was a foot over his head. And if they hadn't been makeing all them errors behind me they wouldn't of been nobody on bases when Zimmerman got that lucky scratch. The serious now stands one and one Al and it is a cinch we will beat them even if they are a bunch of lucky stiffs. They has been great big crowds at both games and it looks like as if we should ought to get over eight hundred dollars a peace if we win and we will win sure because I will beat them three straight if necessary.

But Al I have got bigger news than that for you and I am the happyest man in the world. I told you I had not heard from Hazel for a long time. To-night when I got back to my room they was a letter waiting for me from her.

Al she is married. Maybe you don't know why that makes me happy but I will tell you. She is married to Kid Levy the middle weight. I guess my thirty dollars is gone because in her letter she called me a cheap skate and she inclosed one one-

cent stamp and two twos and said she was paying
me for the glass of beer I once bought her. I
bought her more than that Al but I won't make
no holler. She all so said not for me to never
come near her or her husband would bust my jaw.
I ain't afraid of him or no one else Al but they
ain't no danger of me ever bothering them. She
was no good and I was sorry the minute I agreed
to marry her.

But I was going to tell you why I am happy
or maybe you can guess. Now I can make Violet
my wife and she's got Hazel beat forty ways. She
ain't nowheres near as big as Hazel but she's clas-
sier Al and she will make me a good wife. She
ain't never asked me for no money.

I wrote her a letter the minute I got the good
news and told her to come on over here at once
at my expense. We will be married right after
the serious is over and I want you and Bertha to
be sure and stand up with us. I will wire you at
my own expence the exact date.

It all seems like a dream now about Violet and
I haveing our misunderstanding Al and I don't
see how I ever could of accused her of sending me
that postcard. You and Bertha will be just as
crazy about her as I am when you see her Al. Just
think Al I will be married inside of a week and

to the only girl I ever could of been happy with instead of the woman I never really cared for except as a passing fancy. My happyness would be complete Al if I had not of let that woman steal thirty dollars off of me.

Your happy pal,   JACK.

P. S. Hazel probibly would of insisted on us takeing a trip to Niagara falls or somewheres but I know Violet will be perfectly satisfied if I take her right down to Bedford. Oh you little yellow house.

Chicago, Illinois, October 9.

FRIEND AL: Well Al we have got them beat three games to one now and will wind up the serious to-morrow sure. Callahan sent me in to save poor Allen yesterday and I stopped them dead. But I don't care now Al. I have lost all interest in the game and I don't care if Callahan pitches me to-morrow or not. My heart is just about broke Al and I wouldn't be able to do myself justice feeling the way I do.

I have lost Violet Al and just when I was figureing on being the happyest man in the world. We will get the big money but it won't do me no good. They can keep my share because I won't have no little girl to spend it on.

Her answer to my letter was waiting for me at

home to-night. She is engaged to be married to Joe Hill the big lefthander Jennings got from Providence. Honest Al I don't see how he gets by. He ain't got no more curve ball than a rabbit and his fast one floats up there like a big balloon. He beat us the last game of the regular season here but it was because Callahan had a lot of bushers in the game.

I wish I had knew then that he was stealing my girl and I would of made Callahan pitch me against him. And when he come up to bat I would of beaned him. But I don't suppose you could hurt him by hitting him in the head. The big stiff. Their wedding ain't going to come off till next summer and by that time he will be pitching in the Southwestern Texas League for about fifty dollars a month.

Violet wrote that she wished me all the luck and happyness in the world but it is too late for me to be happy Al and I don't care what kind of luck I have now.

Al you will have to get rid of that lease for me. Fix it up the best way you can. Tell the old man I have changed my plans. I don't know just yet what I will do but maybe I will go to Australia with Mike Donlin's team. If I do I won't care if the boat goes down or not. I don't believe I will even come back to Bedford this winter. It would drive me wild to go past that little house every day and think how happy I might of been.

Maybe I will pitch to-morrow Al and if I do the serious will be over to-morrow night. I can beat them Cubs if I get any kind of decent support. But I don't care now Al.

Yours truly,   JACK.

Chicago, Illinois, October 12.

AL: Your letter received. If the old man won't call it off I guess I will have to try and rent the house to some one else. Do you know of any couple that wants one Al? It looks like I would have to come down there myself and fix things up someway. He is just mean enough to stick me with the house on my hands when I won't have no use for it.

They beat us the day before yesterday as you probibly know and it rained yesterday and to-day. The papers says it will be all O. K. to-morrow and Callahan tells me I am going to work. The Cub pitchers was all shot to peaces and the bad weather is just nuts for them because it will give Cheney a good rest. But I will beat him Al if they don't kick it away behind me.

I must close because I promised Allen the little lefthander that I would come over to his flat and play cards a while to-night and I must wash up and change my collar. Allen's wife's sister is visiting them again and I would give anything not to have to go over there. I am through with girls and don't want nothing to do with them.

I guess it is maybe a good thing it rained to-day because I dreamt about Violet last night and went out and got a couple of high balls before breakfast this morning. I hadn't never drank nothing before breakfast before and it made me kind of sick. But I am all O. K. now.

Your pal,   JACK.

Chicago, Illinois, October 13.

DEAR OLD AL: The serious is all over Al. We are the champions and I done it. I may be home the day after to-morrow or I may not come for a couple of days. I want to see Comiskey before I leave and fix up about my contract for next year. I won't sign for no less than five thousand and if he hands me a contract for less than that I will leave the White Sox flat on their back. I have got over fourteen hundred dollars now Al with the city serious money which was $814.30 and I don't have to worry.

Them reporters will have to give me a square deal this time Al. I had everything and the Cubs done well to score a run. I whiffed Zimmerman three times. Some of the boys say he ain't no hitter but he is a hitter and a good one Al only he could not touch the stuff I got. The umps give them their run because in the fourth inning I had Leach flatfooted off of second base and Weaver tagged him O. K. but the umps wouldn't call it. Then Schulte the lucky stiff happened to get a hold of one and pulled it past first base. I guess Chase must of been asleep. Anyway they scored but I don't care because we piled up six runs on Cheney and I drove in one of them myself with one of the prettiest singles you ever see. It was a spitter and I hit it like a shot. If I had hit it square it would of went out of the park.

Comiskey ought to feel pretty good about me winning and I guess he will give me a contract for anything I want. He will have to or I will go to the Federal League.

We are all invited to a show to-night and I am going with Allen and his wife and her sister Florence. She is O. K. Al and I guess she thinks the same about me. She must because she was out to the game to-day and seen me hand it to

them. She maybe ain't as pretty as Violet and
Hazel but as they say beauty isn't only so deep.

Well Al tell the boys I will be with them soon.
I have gave up the idea of going to Australia because I would have to buy a evening full-dress
suit and they tell me they cost pretty near fifty
dollars.   Yours truly,   JACK.

Chicago, Illinois, October 14.
FRIEND AL: Never mind about that lease. I
want the house after all Al and I have got the
supprise of your life for you.

When I come home to Bedford I will bring
my wife with me. I and Florence fixed things
all up after the show last night and we are going
to be married to-morrow morning. I am a busy
man to-day Al because I have got to get the license
and look round for furniture. And I have also
got to buy some new cloths but they are haveing
a sale on Cottage Grove Avenue at Clark's store
and I know one of the clerks there.

I am the happyest man in the world Al. You
and Bertha and I and Florence will have all kinds
of good times together this winter because I know
Bertha and Florence will like each other. Florence looks something like Bertha at that. I am
glad I didn't get tied up with Violet or Hazel

even if they was a little bit prettier than Florence.

Florence knows a lot about baseball for a girl and you would be supprised to hear her talk. She says I am the best pitcher in the league and she has saw them all. She all so says I am the best looking ball player she ever seen but you know how girls will kid a guy Al. You will like her O. K. I fell for her the first time I seen her.

Your old pal,   JACK.

P. S. I signed up for next year. Comiskey slapped me on the back when I went in to see him and told me I would be a star next year if I took good care of myself. I guess I am a star without waiting for next year Al. My contract calls for twenty-eight hundred a year which is a thousand more than I was getting. And it is pretty near a cinch that I will be in on the World Serious money next season.

P. S. I certainly am relieved about that lease. It would of been fierce to of had that place on my hands all winter and not getting any use out of it. Everything is all O. K. now. Oh you little yellow house.

CHAPTER

3

The Busher's Honeymoon

Chicago, Illinois, October 17.

FRIEND AL: Well Al it looks as if I would not be writeing so much to you now that I am a married man. Yes Al I and Florrie was married the day before yesterday just like I told you we was going to be and Al I am the happyest man in the world though I have spent $30 in the last 3 days incluseive. You was wise Al to get married in Bedford where not nothing is nearly half so dear. My expenses was as follows:

License	$ 2.00
Preist	3.50
Haircut and shave	.35
Shine	.05
Carfair	.45
New suit	14.50
Show tickets	3.00
Flowers	.50
Candy	.30
Hotel	4.50
Tobacco both kinds	.25

You see Al it costs a hole lot of money to get married here. The sum of what I have wrote down is $29.40 but as I told you I have spent $30 and I do not know what I have did with that other $0.60. My new brother-in-law Allen told me I should ought to give the preist $5 and I thought it should be about $2 the same as the license so I split the difference and give him $3.50. I never seen him before and probily won't never see him again so why should I give him anything at all when it is his business to marry couples? But I like to do the right thing. You know me Al.

I thought we would be in Bedford by this time but Florrie wants to say here a few more days because she says she wants to be with her sister. Allen and his wife is thinking about take-ing a flat for the winter instead of going down to Waco Texas where they live. I don't see no sense in that when it costs so much to live here but it is none of my business if they want to throw their money away. But I am glad I got a wife with some sense though she kicked because I did not get no room with a bath which would cost me $2 a day instead of $1.50. I says I guess the clubhouse is still open yet and if I want a bath I can go over there and take the shower. She says Yes and I suppose I can go and jump in the lake. But she would not do that Al because the lake here is cold at this time of the year.

When I told you about my expenses I did not include in it the meals because we would be eating them if I was getting married or not getting married only I have to pay for six meals a day now instead of three and I didn't used to eat no lunch in the playing season except once in a while when I knowed I was not going to work that afternoon. I had a meal ticket which had not quite ran out over to a resturunt on Indiana Ave and we eat there for the first day except at night when I took Allen and his wife to the show with us and then he took us to a chop suye resturunt. I guess you have not never had no chop suye Al and I am here to tell you you have not missed nothing but when Allen was going to buy the supper what could I say? I could not say nothing.

Well yesterday and to-day we been eating at a resturunt on Cottage Grove Ave near the hotel and at the resturunt on Indiana that I had the meal ticket at only I do not like to buy no new meal ticket when I am not going to be round here no more than a few days. Well Al I guess the meals has cost me all together about $1.50 and I have eat very little myself. Florrie always wants

desert ice cream or something and that runs up
into money faster than regular stuff like stake and
ham and eggs.

Well Al Florrie says it is time for me to keep
my promise and take her to the moveing pictures
which is $0.20 more because the one she likes
round here costs a dime apeace. So I must close
for this time and will see you soon.

Your pal,   JACK.

Chicago, Illinois, October 22.

AL: Just a note Al to tell you why I have not
yet came to Bedford yet where I expected I would
be long before this time. Allen and his wife have
took a furnished flat for the winter and Allen's
wife wants Florrie to stay here untill they get
settled. Meentime it is costing me a hole lot of
money at the hotel and for meals besides I am
paying $10 a month rent for the house you got
for me and what good am I getting out of it? But
Florrie wants to help her sister and what can I
say? Though I did make her promise she would
not stay no longer than next Saturday at least.
So I guess Al we will be home on the evening train
Saturday and then may be I can save some money.

I know Al that you and Bertha will like Florrie
when you get acquainted with her spesially Bertha

though Florrie dresses pretty swell and spends a hole lot of time fusing with her face and her hair.

She says to me to-night Who are you writing to and I told her Al Blanchard who I have told you about a good many times. She says I bet you are writing to some girl and acted like as though she was kind of jealous. So I thought I would tease her a little and I says I don't know no girls except you and Violet and Hazel. Who is Violet and Hazel? she says. I kind of laughed and says Oh I guess I better not tell you and then she says I guess you will tell me. That made me kind of mad because no girl can't tell me what to do. She says Are you going to tell me? and I says No.

Then she says If you don't tell me I will go over to Marie's that is her sister Allen's wife and stay all night. I says Go on and she went downstairs but I guess she probily went to get a soda because she has some money of her own that I give her. This was about two hours ago and she is probily down in the hotel lobby now trying to scare me by makeing me believe she has went to her sister's. But she can't fool me Al and I am now going out to mail this letter and get a beer. I won't never tell her about Violet and Hazel if she is going to act like that.

Yours truly,   JACK.

Chicago, Illinois, October 24.

FRIEND AL: I guess I told you Al that we would be home Saturday evening. I have changed my mind. Allen and his wife has a spair bedroom and wants us to come there and stay a week or two. It won't cost nothing except they will probily want to go out to the moveing pictures nights and we will probily have to go along with them and I am a man Al that wants to pay his share and not be cheap.

I and Florrie had our first quarrle the other night. I guess I told you the start of it but I don't remember. I made some crack about Violet and Hazel just to tease Florrie and she wanted to know who they was and I would not tell her. So she gets sore and goes over to Marie's to stay all night. I was just kidding Al and was willing to tell her about them two poor girls whatever she wanted to know except that I don't like to brag about girls being stuck on me. So I goes over to Marie's after her and tells her all about them except that I turned them down cold at the last minute to marry her because I did not want her to get all swelled up. She made me sware that I did not never care nothing about them and that was easy because it was the truth. So she

come back to the hotel with me just like I knowed
she would when I ordered her to.

They must not be no mistake about who is the
boss in my house. Some men lets their wife run
all over them but I am not that kind. You know
me Al.

I must get busy and pack my suitcase if I am
going to move over to Allen's. I sent three col-
lars and a shirt to the laundrey this morning so
even if we go over there to-night I will have to
take another trip back this way in a day or two.
I won't mind Al because they sell my kind of beer
down to the corner and I never seen it sold nowheres else in Chi. You know the kind it is,
eh Al? I wish I was lifting a few with you to-
night.   Your pal,   JACK.

Chicago, Illinois, October 28.

DEAR OLD AL: Florrie and Marie has went
downtown shopping because Florrie thinks she has
got to have a new dress though she has got two
changes of cloths now and I don't know what she
can do with another one. I hope she don't find
none to suit her though it would not hurt none
if she got something for next spring at a reduck-
shon. I guess she must think I am Charles A.
Comiskey or somebody. Allen has went to a col-

ledge football game.   One of the reporters give
him a pass.   I don't see nothing in football except
a lot of scrapping between little slobs that I could
lick the whole bunch of them so I did not care to
go.   The reporter is one of the guys that travled
round with our club all summer.   He called up
and said he hadn't only the one pass but he was
not hurting my feelings none because I would not
go to no rotten football game if they payed me.

The flat across the hall from this here one is for
rent furnished.   They want $40 a month for it
and I guess they think they must be lots of suckers
running round loose.   Marie was talking about
it and says Why don't you and Florrie take it and
then we can be right together all winter long and
have some big times?   Florrie says It would be
all right with me.   What about it Jack?   I says
What do you think I am?   I don't have to live
in no high price flat when I got a home in Bedford
where they ain't no people trying to hold everybody up all the time.   So they did not say no
more about it when they seen I was in ernest.
Nobody cannot tell me where I am going to live
sister-in-law or no sister-in-law.   If I was to rent
the rotten old flat I would be paying $50 a month
rent includeing the house down in Bedford.   Fine
chance Al.

Well Al I am lonesome and thirsty so more later.   Your pal,   JACK.

Chicago, Illinois, November 2.

FRIEND AL: Well Al I got some big news for you. I am not comeing to Bedford this winter after all except to make a visit which I guess will be round Xmas. I changed my mind about that flat across the hall from the Allens and decided to take it after all. The people who was in it and owns the furniture says they would let us have it till the 1 of May if we would pay $42.50 a month which is only $2.50 a month more than they would of let us have it for for a short time. So you see we got a bargain because it is all furnished and everything and we won't have to blow no money on furniture besides the club goes to California the middle of Febuery so Florrie would not have no place to stay while I am away.

The Allens only subleased their flat from some other people till the 2 of Febuery and when I and Allen goes West Marie can come over and stay with Florrie so you see it is best all round. If we should of boughten furniture it would cost us in the neighborhood of $100 even without no piano and they is a piano in this here flat which makes it nice because Florrie plays pretty good with one hand and we can have lots of good times at home without it costing us nothing except just the bear liveing expenses. I consider myself lucky to of found out about this before it was too late and somebody else had of gotten the tip.

Now Al old pal I want to ask a great favor of you Al. I all ready have payed one month rent $10 on the house in Bedford and I want you to see the old man and see if he won't call off that lease. Why should I be paying $10 a month rent down there and $42.50 up here when the house down there is not no good to me because I am liveing up here all winter? See Al? Tell him I will gladly give him another month rent to call off the lease but don't tell him that if you don't have to. I want to be fare with him.

If you will do this favor for me, Al, I won't never forget it. Give my kindest to Bertha and tell her I am sorry I and Florrie won't see her right away but you see how it is Al.

Yours,   JACK.

Chicago, Illinois, November 30.

FRIEND AL: I have not wrote for a long time have I Al but I have been very busy. They was not enough furniture in the flat and we have been buying some more. They was enough for some

people maybe but I and Florrie is the kind that
won't have nothing but the best. The furniture
them people had in the liveing room was oak but
they had a bookcase bilt in in the flat that was
mohoggeny and Florrie would not stand for no
joke combination like that so she moved the oak
chairs and table in to the spair bedroom and we
went downtown to buy some mohoggeny. But it
costs too much Al and we was feeling pretty bad
about it when we seen some Sir Cashion walnut
that was prettier even than the mohoggeny and
not near so expensive. It is not no real Sir Cashion
walnut but it is just as good and we got it reasonable. Then we got some mission chairs for the
dining room because the old ones was just straw
and was no good and we got a big lether couch for
$9 that somebody can sleep on if we get to much
company.

I hope you and Bertha can come up for the holidays and see how comfertible we are fixed. That
is all the new furniture we have boughten but
Florrie set her heart on some old Rose drapes and
a red table lamp that is the biggest you ever seen
Al and I did not have the heart to say no. The
hole thing cost me in the neighborhood of $110
which is very little for what we got and then it
will always be ourn even when we move away

from this flat though we will have to leave the furniture that belongs to the other people but their part of it is not no good anyway.

I guess I told you Al how much money I had when the season ended. It was $1400 all told includeing the city serious money. Well Al I got in the neighborhood of $800 left because I give $200 to Florrie to send down to Texas to her other sister who had a bad egg for a husband that managed a club in the Texas Oklahoma League and this was the money she had to pay to get the divorce. I am glad Al that I was lucky enough to marry happy and get a good girl for my wife that has got some sense and besides if I have got $800 left I should not worry as they say.

Your pal,   JACK.

Chicago, Illinois, December 7.

DEAR OLD AL: No I was in ernest Al when I says that I wanted you and Bertha to come up here for the holidays. I know I told you that I might come to Bedford for the holidays but that is all off. I have gave up the idea of comeing to Bedford for the holidays and I want you to be sure and come up here for the holidays and I will show you a good time. I would love to have Bertha come to and she can come if she wants to only Florrie don't know if she would have a good time or not and thinks maybe she would rather stay in Bedford and you come alone. But be sure and have Bertha come if she wants to come but maybe she would not injoy it. You know best Al.

I don't think the old man give me no square deal on that lease but if he wants to stick me all right. I am grateful to you Al for trying to fix it up but maybe you could of did better if you had of went at it in a different way. I am not finding no fault with my old pal though. Don't think that. When I have a pal I am the man to stick to him threw thick and thin. If the old man is going to hold me to that lease I guess I will have to stand it and I guess I won't starv to death for no $10 a month because I am going to get $2800 next year besides the city serious money and maybe we will get into the World Serious too. I know we will if Callahan will pitch me every 3d day like I wanted him to last season. But if you had of approached the old man in a different way maybe you could of fixed it up. I wish you would try it again Al if it is not no trouble.

We had Allen and his wife here for thanksgiveing dinner and the dinner cost me better than $5. I thought we had enough to eat to last a week but about six o'clock at night Florrie and Marie said they was hungry and we went downtown and had dinner all over again and I payed for it and it cost me $5 more. Allen was all ready to pay for it when Florrie said No this day's treat is on us so I had to pay for it but I don't see why she did not wait and let me do the talking. I was going to pay for it any way.

Be sure and come and visit us for the holidays Al and of coarse if Bertha wants to come bring her along. We will be glad to see you both. I won't never go back on a friend and pal. You know me Al.   Your old pal,   JACK.

Chicago, Illinois, December 20.

FRIEND AL: I don't see what can be the matter with Bertha because you know Al we would not care how she dressed and would not make no kick if she come up here in a night gown. She did not have no license to say we was to swell for her because we did not never think of nothing like that. I wish you would talk to her again Al and tell her she need not get sore on me and that both her and you is welcome at my house any time I ask you to come. See if you can't make her change her mind Al because I feel like as if she must of took offense at something I may of wrote you. I am sorry you and her are not comeing but I suppose you know best. Only we was getting all ready for you and Florrie said only the other day that she wished the holidays was over but that was before she knowed you was not comeing. I hope you can come Al.

Well Al I guess there is not no use talking to the old man no more. You have did the best you could but I wish I could of came down there and talked to him. I will pay him his rotten old $10 a month and the next time I come to Bedford and meet him on the street I will bust his jaw. I know he is a old man Al but I don't like to see nobody get the best of me and I am sorry I ever asked him to let me off. Some of them old skinflints has no heart Al but why should I fight with a old man over chicken feed like $10? Florrie says a star pitcher like I should not ought never to scrap about little things and I guess she is right Al so I will pay the old man his $10 a month if I have to.

Florrie says she is jealous of me writeing to you so much and she says she would like to meet this great old pal of mine. I would like to have her meet you to Al and I would like to have you change your mind and come and visit us and I am sorry you can't come Al.

Yours truly,   JACK.

Chicago, Illinois, December 27.

OLD PAL: I guess all these lefthanders is alike though I thought this Allen had some sense. I thought he was different from the most and was not no rummy but they are all alike Al and they are all lucky that somebody don't hit them over the head with a ax and kill them but I guess at that you could not hurt no lefthanders by hitting them over the head. We was all down on State St. the day before Xmas and the girls was all tired out and ready to go home but Allen says No I guess we better stick down a while because now the crowds is out and it will be fun to watch them. So we walked up and down State St. about a hour longer and finally we come in front of a big jewlry store window and in it was a swell dimond ring that was marked $100. It was a ladies' ring so Marie says to Allen Why don't you buy that for me? And Allen says Do you really want it? And she says she did.

So we tells the girls to wait and we goes over to a salloon where Allen has got a friend and gets a check cashed and we come back and he bought the ring. Then Florrie looks like as though she was getting all ready to cry and I asked her what was the matter and she says I had not boughten her no ring not even when we was engaged. So

I and Allen goes back to the salloon and I gets a check cashed and we come back and bought another ring but I did not think the ring Allen had boughten was worth no $100 so I gets one for $75. Now Al you know I am not makeing no kick on spending a little money for a present for my own wife but I had allready boughten her a rist watch for $15 and a rist watch was just what she had wanted. I was willing to give her the ring if she had not of wanted the rist watch more than the ring but when I give her the ring I kept the rist watch and did not tell her nothing about it.

Well I come downtown alone the day after Xmas and they would not take the rist watch back in the store where I got it. So I am going to give it to her for a New Year's present and I guess that will make Allen feel like a dirty doose. But I guess you cannot hurt no lefthander's feelings at that. They are all alike. But Allen has not got nothing but a dinky curve ball and a fast ball that looks like my slow one. If Comiskey was not good hearted he would of sold him long ago.

I sent you and Bertha a cut glass dish Al which was the best I could get for the money and it was pretty high pricet at that. We was glad to get the pretty pincushions from you and Bertha and Florrie says to tell you that we are well supplied

with pincushions now because the ones you sent
makes a even half dozen. Thanks Al for remem-
bering us and thank Bertha too though I guess you
paid for them.   Your pal,   Jack.

Chicago, Illinois, Januery 3.
Old Pal: Al I been pretty sick ever since New
Year's eve. We had a table at 1 of the swell
resturunts downtown and I never seen so much
wine drank in my life. I would rather of had
beer but they would not sell us none so I found
out that they was a certain kind that you can get
for $1 a bottle and it is just as good as the kind
that has got all them fancy names but this left-
hander starts ordering some other kind about 11
oclock and it was $5 a bottle and the girls both
says they liked it better. I could not see a hole
lot of difference myself and I would of gave $0.20
for a big stine of my kind of beer. You know
me Al. Well Al you know they is not nobody
that can drink.more than your old pal and I was
all O. K. at one oclock but I seen the girls was
getting kind of sleepy so I says we better go home.
Then Marie says Oh, shut up and don't be no
quiter. I says You better shut up yourself and
not be telling me to shut up, and she says What
will you do if I don't shut up? And I says I

would bust her in the jaw. But you know Al I
would not think of busting no girl. Then Florrie
says You better not start nothing because you had
to much to drink or you would not be talking
about busting girls in the jaw. Then I says I
don't care if it is a girl I bust or a lefthander.
I did not mean nothing at all Al but Marie says
I had insulted Allen and he gets up and slaps my
face. Well Al I am not going to stand that from
nobody not even if he is my brother-in-law and
a lefthander that has not got enough speed to
brake a pain of glass.

So I give him a good beating and the waiters
butts in and puts us all out for fighting and I
and Florrie comes home in a taxi and Allen and
his wife don't get in till about 5 oclock so I guess
she must of had to of took him to a doctor to get
fixed up. I been in bed ever since till just this
morning kind of sick to my stumach. I guess I
must of eat something that did not agree with me.
Allen come over after breakfast this morning and
asked me was I all right so I guess he is not sore
over the beating I give him or else he wants to
make friends because he has saw that I am a bad
guy to monkey with.

Florrie tells me a little while ago that she paid
the hole bill at the resturunt with my money be-

cause Allen was broke so you see what kind of a
cheap skate he is Al and some day I am going to
bust his jaw. She won't tell me how much the
bill was and I won't ask her to no more because
we had a good time outside of the fight and what
do I care if we spent a little money?

Yours truly,   JACK.

Chicago, Illinois, January 20.

FRIEND AL: Allen and his wife have gave up
the flat across the hall from us and come over
to live with us because we got a spair bedroom
and why should they not have the bennifit of it?
But it is pretty hard for the girls to have to cook
and do the work when they is four of us so I
have a hired girl who does it all for $7 a week.
It is great stuff Al because now we can go round
as we please and don't have to wait for no dishes
to be washed or nothing. We generally almost
always has dinner downtown in the evening so
it is pretty soft for the girl too. She don't generally have no more than one meal to get because
we generally run round downtown till late and
don't get up till about noon.

That sounds funny don't it Al, when I used to
get up at 5 every morning down home. Well Al
I can tell you something else that may sound

funny and that is that I lost my taste for beer.
I don't seem to care for it no more and I found
I can stand allmost as many drinks of other stuff
as I could of beer.   I guess Al they is not nobody
ever lived can drink more and stand up better
under it than me.   I make the girls and Allen
quit every night.

I only got just time to write you this short note
because Florrie and Marie is giving a big party
to-night and I and Allen have got to beat it out
of the house and stay out of the way till they get
things ready.   It is Marie's berthday and she says
she is 22 but say Al if she is 22 Kid Gleason is
30.   Well Al the girls says we must blow so I
will run out and mail this letter.

Yours truly,   JACK.

Chicago, Illinois, January 31.

AL: Allen is going to take Marie with him
on the training trip to California and of course
Florrie has been at me to take her along.   I told
her postivly that she can't go.   I can't afford no
stunt like that but still I am up against it to know
what to do with her while we are on the trip because Marie won't be here to stay with her.   I
don't like to leave her here all alone but they is
nothing to it Al I can't afford to take her along.

She says I don't see why you can't take me if Allen takes Marie. And I says That stuff is all O. K. for Allen because him and Marie has been grafting off of us all winter. And then she gets mad and tells me I should not ought to say her sister was no grafter. I did not mean nothing like that Al but you don't never know when a woman is going to take offense.

If our furniture was down in Bedford everything would be all O. K. because I could leave her there and I would feel all O. K. because I would know that you and Bertha would see that she was getting along O. K. But they would not be no sense in sending her down to a house that has not no furniture in it. I wish I knowed somewheres where she could visit Al. I would be willing to pay her bord even.

Well Al enough for this time.

Your old pal,   JACK.

Chicago, Illinois, Febuery 4.

FRIEND AL: You are a real old pal Al and I certainly am greatful to you for the invatation. I have not told Florrie about it yet but I am sure she will be tickled to death and it is certainly kind of you old pal. I did not never dream of nothing like that. I note what you say Al about not excepting no bord but I think it would be better and I would feel better if you would take something say about $2 a week.

I know Bertha will like Florrie and that they will get along O. K. together because Florrie can learn her how to make her cloths look good and fix her hair and fix up her face. I feel like as if you had took a big load off of me Al and I won't never forget it.

If you don't think I should pay no bord for Florrie all right. Suit yourself about that old pal.

We are leaveing here the 20 of Febuery and if you don't mind I will bring Florrie down to you about the 18. I would like to see the old bunch again and spesially you and Bertha.

Yours,   JACK.

P. S. We will only be away till April 14 and that is just a nice visit. I wish we did not have no flat on our hands.

Chicago, Illinois, Febuery 9.

OLD PAL: I want to thank you for asking Florrie to come down there and visit you Al but I find she can't get away. I did not know she had no engagements but she says she may go down to her folks in Texas and she don't want to say that she will come to visit you when it is so indefanate. So thank you just the same Al and thank Bertha too.

Florrie is still at me to take her along to California but honest Al I can't do it. I am right down to my last $50 and I have not payed no rent for this month. I owe the hired girl 2 weeks' salery and both I and Florrie needs some new cloths.

Florrie has just came in since I started writeing this letter and we have been talking some more about California and she says maybe if I would ask Comiskey he would take her along as the club's guest. I had not never thought of that Al and maybe he would because he is a pretty good scout and I guess I will go and see him about it. The league has its skedule meeting here to-morrow and may be I can see him down to the hotel where they meet at. I am so worried Al that I can't write no more but I will tell you how I come out with Comiskey.

Your pal,   Jack.

Chicago, Illinois, Febuery 11.

Friend Al: I am up against it right Al and I don't know where I am going to head in at. I went down to the hotel where the league was

holding its skedule meeting at and I seen Comiskey and got some money off of the club but I owe
all the money I got off of them and I am still
wondering what to do about Florrie.

Comiskey was busy in the meeting when I went
down there and they was not no chance to see
him for a while so I and Allen and some of the
boys hung round and had a few drinks and
fanned. This here Joe Hill the busher that Detroit has got that Violet is hooked up to was round
the hotel. I don't know what for but I felt like
busting his jaw only the boys told me I had better not do nothing because I might kill him and
any way he probily won't be in the league much
longer. Well finally Comiskey got threw the
meeting and I seen him and he says Hello young
man what can I do for you? And I says I would
like to get $100 advance money. He says Have
you been takeing care of yourself down in Bedford? And I told him I had been liveing here
all winter and it did not seem to make no hit with
him though I don't see what business it is of hisn
where I live.

So I says I had been takeing good care of myself. And I have Al. You know that. So he
says I should come to the ball park the next day
which is to-day and he would have the secretary

take care of me but I says I could not wait and
so he give me $100 out of his pocket and says he
would have it charged against my salery. I was
just going to brace him about the California trip
when he got away and went back to the meeting.

Well Al I hung round with the bunch waiting
for him to get threw again and we had some
more drinks and finally Comiskey was threw again
and I braced him in the lobby and asked him if
it was all right to take my wife along to California. He says Sure they would be glad to have
her along. And then I says Would the club pay
her fair? He says I guess you must of spent that
$100 buying some nerve. He says Have you not
got no sisters that would like to go along to? He
says Does your wife insist on the drawing room
or will she take a lower birth? He says Is my
special train good enough for her?

Then he turns away from me and I guess some
of the boys must of heard the stuff he pulled
because they was laughing when he went away
but I did not see nothing to laugh at. But I guess
he ment that I would have to pay her fair if she
goes along and that is out of the question Al. I
am up against it and I don't know where I am
going to head in at.   Your pal,   JACK.

Chicago, Illinois, Febuery 12.

DEAR OLD AL: I guess everything will be all
O. K. now at least I am hopeing it will. When
I told Florrie about how I come out with Comiskey she bawled her head off and I thought for
a while I was going to have to call a doctor or
something but pretty soon she cut it out and we
sat there a while without saying nothing. Then
she says If you could get your salery razed a
couple of hundred dollars a year would you borrow the money ahead somewheres and take me
along to California? I says Yes I would if I
could get a couple hundred dollars more salery
but how could I do that when I had signed a
contract for $2800 last fall allready? She says
Don't you think you are worth more than $2800?
And I says Yes of coarse I was worth more than
$2800. She says Well if you will go and talk
the right way to Comiskey I believe he will give
you $3000 but you must be sure you go at it the
right way and don't go and ball it all up.

Well we argude about it a while because I
don't want to hold nobody up Al but finally I
says I would. It would not be holding nobody
up anyway because I am worth $3000 to the club
if I am worth a nichol. The papers is all saying
that the club has got a good chance to win the

pennant this year and talking about the pitching staff and I guess they would not be no pitching staff much if it was not for I and one or two others—about one other I guess.

So it looks like as if everything will be all O. K. now Al. I am going to the office over to the park to see him the first thing in the morning and I am pretty sure that I will get what I am after because if I do not he will see that I am going to quit and then he will see what he is up against and not let me get away.

I will let you know how I come out.

Your pal,   Jack.

Chicago, Illinois, Febuery 14.

Friend Al: Al old pal I have got a big suprise for you. I am going to the Federal League. I had a run in with Comiskey yesterday and I guess I told him a thing or 2. I guess he would of been glad to sign me at my own figure before I got threw but I was so mad I would not give him no chance to offer me another contract.

I got out to the park at 9 oclock yesterday morning and it was a hour before he showed up and then he kept me waiting another hour so I was pretty sore when I finally went in to see him. He says Well young man what can I do for you?

I says I come to see about my contract. He says
Do you want to sign up for next year all ready?
I says No I am talking about this year. He says
I thought I and you talked business last fall. And
I says 'Yes but now I think I am worth more
money and I want to sign a contract for $3000.
He says If you behave yourself and work good
this year I will see that you are took care of. But
I says That won't do because I have got to be sure
I am going to get $3000.

Then he says I am not sure you are going to get
anything. I says What do you mean? And he
says I have gave you a very fare contract and if
you don't want to live up to it that is your own
business. So I give him a awful call Al and told
him I would jump to the Federal League. He
says Oh, I would not do that if I was you. They
are haveing a hard enough time as it is. So I says
something back to him and he did not say nothing
to me and I beat it out of the office.

I have not told Florrie about the Federal
League business yet as I am going to give her a
big supprise. I bet they will take her along with
me on the training trip and pay her fair but even
if they don't I should not worry because I will
make them give me a contract for $4000 a year

and then I can afford to take her with me on all
the trips.

I will go down and see Tinker to-morrow morning and I will write you to-morrow night Al how
much salery they are going to give me. But I
won't sign for no less than $4000. You know
me Al.   Yours,   JACK.

Chicago, Illinois, Febuery 15.

OLD PAL: It is pretty near midnight Al but
I been to bed a couple of times and I can't get
no sleep. I am worried to death Al and I don't
know where I am going to head in at. Maybe
I will go out and buy a gun Al and end it all and
I guess it would be better for everybody. But
I cannot do that Al because I have not got the
money to buy a gun with.

I went down to see Tinker about signing up
with the Federal League and he was busy in the
office when I come in. Pretty soon Buck Perry
the pitcher that was with Boston last year come
out and seen me and as Tinker was still busy we
went out and had a drink together. Buck shows
me a contract for $5000 a year and Tinker had
allso gave him a $500 bonus. So pretty soon I
went up to the office and pretty soon Tinker seen
me and called me into his private office and asked

what did I want. I says I was ready to jump
for $4000 and a bonus. He says I thought you
was signed up with the White Sox. I says Yes I
was but I was not satisfied. He says That does
not make no difference to me if you are satisfied
or not. You ought to of came to me before you
signed a contract. I says I did not know enough
but I know better now. He says Well it is to
late now. We cannot have nothing to do with
you because you have went and signed a contract
with the White Sox. I argude with him a while
and asked him to come out and have a drink so
we could talk it over but he said he was busy so
they was nothing for me to do but blow.

So I am not going to the Federal League Al and
I will not go with the White Sox because I have
got a raw deal. Comiskey will be sorry for what
he done when his team starts the season and is
up against it for good pitchers and then he will
probily be willing to give me anything I ask for
but that don't do me no good now Al. I am way
in debt and no chance to get no money from nobody. I wish I had of stayed with Terre Haute
Al and never saw this league.

Your pal,   JACK.

Chicago, Illinois, Febuery 17.

FRIEND AL: Al don't never let nobody tell you that these here lefthanders is right. This Allen my own brother-in-law who married sisters has been grafting and spongeing on me all winter Al. Look what he done to me now Al. You know how hard I been up against it for money and I know he has got plenty of it because I seen it on him. Well Al I was scared to tell Florrie I was cleaned out and so I went to Allen yesterday and says I had to have $100 right away because I owed the rent and owed the hired girl's salery and could not even pay no grocery bill. And he says No he could not let me have none because he has got to save all his money to take his wife on the trip to California. And here he has been liveing on me all winter and maybe I could of took my wife to California if I had not of spent all my money takeing care of this no good lefthander and his wife. And Al honest he has not got a thing and ought not to be in the league. He gets by with a dinky curve ball and has not got no more smoke than a rabbit or something.

Well Al I felt like busting him in the jaw but then I thought No I might kill him and then I would have Marie and Florrie both to take care of

and God knows one of them is enough besides paying his funeral expenses. So I walked away from
him without takeing a crack at him and went into
the other room where Florrie and Marie was at.
I says to Marie I says Marie I wish you would go
in the other room a minute because I want to talk
to Florrie. So Marie beats it into the other room
and then I tells Florrie all about what Comiskey
and the Federal League done to me. She bawled
something awful and then she says I was no good
and she wished she had not never married me.
I says I wisht it too and then she says Do you
mean that and starts to cry.

I told her I was sorry I says that because they
is not no use fusing with girls Al specially when
they is your wife. She says No California trip
for me and then she says What are you going
to do? And I says I did not know. She says
Well if I was a man I would do something. So
then I got mad and I says I will do something.
So I went down to the corner salloon and started
in to get good and drunk but I could not do it
Al because I did not have the money.

Well old pal I am going to ask you a big favor
and it is this I want you to send me $100 Al for
just a few days till I can get on my feet. I do
not know when I can pay it back Al but I guess

you know the money is good and I know you have got it. Who would not have it when they live in Bedford? And besides I let you take $20 in June 4 years ago Al and you give it back but I would not have said nothing to you if you had of kept it. Let me hear from you right away old pal.   Yours truly,   JACK.

Chicago, Illinois, Febuery 19.

AL: I am certainly greatful to you Al for the $100 which come just a little while ago. I will pay the rent with it and part of the grocery bill and I guess the hired girl will have to wait a while for hern but she is sure to get it because I don't never forget my debts. I have changed my mind about the White Sox and I am going to go on the trip and take Florrie along because I don't think it would not be right to leave her here alone in Chi when her sister and all of us is going.

I am going over to the ball park and up in the office pretty soon to see about it. I will tell Comiskey I changed my mind and he will be glad to get me back because the club has not got no chance to finish nowheres without me. But I won't go on no trip or give the club my services without them giveing me some more advance money so as I can take Florrie along with me because Al I would not go without her.

Maybe Comiskey will make my salery $3000 like I wanted him to when he sees I am willing to be a good fellow and go along with him and when he knows that the Federal League would of gladly gave me $4000 if I had not of signed no contract with the White Sox.

I think I will ask him for $200 advance money Al and if I get it may be I can send part of your $100 back to you but I know you cannot be in no hurry Al though you says you wanted it back as soon as possible. You could not be very hard up Al because it don't cost near so much to live in Bedford as it does up here.

Anyway I will let you know how I come out with Comiskey and I will write you as soon as I get out to Paso Robles if I don't get no time to write you before I leave.

Your pal,   JACK.

P. S.   I have took good care of myself all winter Al and I guess I ought to have a great season.

P. S.   Florrie is tickled to death about going along and her and I will have some time together out there on the Coast if I can get some money somewheres.

Chicago, Illinois, Febuery 21.

FRIEND AL: I have not got the heart to write this letter to you Al. I am up here in my $42.50 a month flat and the club has went to California and Florrie has went too. I am flat broke Al and all I am asking you is to send me enough money to pay my fair to Bedford and they and all their leagues can go to hell Al.

I was out to the ball park early yesterday morning and some of the boys was there allready fanning and kidding each other. They tried to kid me to when I come in but I guess I give them as good as they give me. I was not in no mind for kidding Al because I was there on business and I wanted to see Comiskey and get it done with.

Well the secretary come in finally and I went up to him and says I wanted to see Comiskey right away. He says The boss was busy and what did I want to see him about and I says I wanted to get some advance money because I was going to take my wife on the trip. He says This would be a fine time to be telling us about it even if you was going on the trip.

And I says What do you mean? And he says You are not going on no trip with us because we have got wavers on you and you are sold to Milwaukee.

Honest Al I thought he was kidding at first and I was waiting for him to laugh but he did not laugh and finally I says What do you mean? And he says Cannot you understand no English? You are sold to Milwaukee. Then I says I want to see the boss. He says It won't do you no good to see the boss and he is to busy to see you. I says I want to get some money. And he says You cannot get no money from this club and all you get is your fair to Milwaukee. I says I am not going to no Milwaukee anyway and he says I should not worry about that. Suit yourself.

Well Al I told some of the boys about it and they was pretty sore and says I ought to bust the secretary in the jaw and I was going to do it when I thought No I better not because he is a little guy and I might kill him.

I looked all over for Kid Gleason but he was not nowheres round and they told me he would not get into town till late in the afternoon. If I could of saw him Al he would of fixed me all up. I asked 3 or 4 of the boys for some money but they says they was all broke.

But I have not told you the worst of it yet Al. When I come back to the flat Allen and Marie and Florrie was busy packing up and they asked me how I come out. I told them and Allen just stood there stareing like a big rummy but Marie and Florrie both begin to cry and I almost felt like as if I would like to cry to only I am not no baby Al.

Well Al I told Florrie she might just is well quit packing and make up her mind that she was not going nowheres till I got money enough to go to Bedford where I belong. She kept right on crying and it got so I could not stand it no more so I went out to get a drink because I still had just about a dollar left yet.

It was about 2 oclock when I left the flat and pretty near 5 when I come back because I had ran in to some fans that knowed who I was and would not let me get away and besides I did not want to see no more of Allen and Marie till they was out of the house and on their way.

But when I come in Al they was nobody there. They was not nothing there except the furniture and a few of my things scattered round. I sit down for a few minutes because I guess I must of had to much to drink but finally I seen a note on the table addressed to me and I seen it was Florrie's writeing.

I do not remember just what was there in the note Al because I tore it up the minute I read it but it was something about I could not support no wife and Allen had gave her enough money to go back to Texas and she was going on the 6 oclock train and it would not do me no good to try and stop her.

Well Al they was not no danger of me trying to stop her. She was not no good Al and I wisht I had not of never saw either she or her sister or my brother-in-law.

For a minute I thought I would follow Allen and his wife down to the deepo where the special train was to pull out of and wait till I see him and punch his jaw but I seen that would not get me nothing.

So here I am all alone Al and I will have to stay here till you send me the money to come home. You better send me $25 because I have got a few little debts I should ought to pay before I leave town. I am not going to Milwaukee Al because I did not get no decent deal and nobody cannot make no sucker out of me.

Please hurry up with the $25 Al old friend because I am sick and tired of Chi and want to get back there with my old pal.

Yours,   JACK.

P. S.   Al I wish I had of took poor little Violet when she was so stuck on me.

CHAPTER

4

A New Busher Breaks In

Chicago, Illinois, March 2.

FRIEND AL: Al that peace in the paper was all O. K. and the right dope just like you said. I seen president Johnson the president of the league to-day and he told me the peace in the papers was the right dope and Comiskey did not have no right to sell me to Milwaukee because the Detroit Club had never gave no wavers on me. He says the Detroit Club was late in fileing their claim and Comiskey must of tooken it for granted that they was going to wave but president Johnson was pretty sore about it at that and says Comiskey did not have no right to sell me till he was positive that they was not no team that wanted me.

It will probily cost Comiskey some money for acting like he done and not paying no attention to the rules and I would not be supprised if president Johnson had him throwed out of the league.

Well I asked president Johnson should I re-

port at once to the Detroit Club down south and
he says No you better wait till you hear from
Comiskey and I says What has Comiskey got to
do with it now? And he says Comiskey will
own you till he sells you to Detroit or somewheres else. So I will have to go out to the ball
park to-morrow and see is they any mail for me
there because I probily will get a letter from
Comiskey telling me I am sold to Detroit.

If I had of thought at the time I would of
knew that Detroit never would give no wavers
on me after the way I showed Cobb and Crawford up last fall and I might of knew too that
Detroit is in the market for good pitchers because
they got a rotten pitching staff but they won't
have no rotten staff when I get with them.

If necessary I will pitch every other day for
Jennings and if I do we will win the pennant
sure because Detroit has got a club that can get
2 or 3 runs every day and all as I need to win
most of my games is 1 run. I can't hardly wait
till Jennings works me against the White Sox and
what I will do to them will be a plenty. It don't
take no pitching to beat them anyway and when
they get up against a pitcher like I they might as
well leave their bats in the bag for all the good
their bats will do them.

I guess Cobb and Crawford will be glad to have me on the Detroit Club because then they won't never have to hit against me except in practice and I won't pitch my best in practice because they will be teammates of mine and I don't never like to show none of my teammates up. At that though I don't suppose Jennings will let me do much pitching in practice because when he gets a hold of a good pitcher he won't want me to take no chances of throwing my arm away in practice.

Al just think how funny it will be to have me pitching for the Tigers in the same town where Violet lives and pitching on the same club with her husband. It will not be so funny for Violet and her husband though because when she has a chance to see me work regular she will find out what a mistake she made takeing that left-hander instead of a man that has got some future and soon will be makeing 5 or $6000 a year because I won't sign with Detroit for no less than $5000 at most. Of coarse I could of had her if I had of wanted to but still and all it will make her feel pretty sick to see me winning games for Detroit while her husband is batting fungos and getting splinters in his unie from slideing up and down the bench.

As for her husband the first time he opens his

clam to me I will haul off and bust him one in
the jaw but I guess he will know more than to
start trouble with a man of my size and who is
going to be one of their stars while he is just
holding down a job because they feel sorry for
him. I wish he could of got the girl I married
instead of the one he got and I bet she would of
drove him crazy. But I guess you can't drive a
left-hander crazyer than he is to begin with.

I have not heard nothing from Florrie Al and
I don't want to hear nothing. I and her is better
apart and I wish she would sew me for a bill of
divorce so she could not go round claiming she
is my wife and disgraceing my name. If she
would consent to sew me for a bill of divorce I
would gladly pay all the expenses and settle with
her for any sum of money she wants say about
$75.00 or $100.00 and they is no reason I should
give her a nichol after the way her and her sister
Marie and her brother-in-law Allen grafted off
of me. Probily I could sew her for a bill of
divorce but they tell me it costs money to sew
and if you just lay low and let the other side do
the sewing it don't cost you a nichol.

It is pretty late Al and I have got to get up
early to-morrow and go to the ball park and see

is they any mail for me. I will let you know
what I hear old pal.

Your old pal,   Jack.

Chicago, Illinois, March 4.

Al: I am up against it again. I went out to
the ball park office yesterday and they was nobody there except John somebody who is asst
secretary and all the rest of them is out on the
Coast with the team. Maybe this here John was
trying to kid me but this is what he told me.
First I says Is they a letter here for me? And
he says No. And I says I was expecting word
from Comiskey that I should join the Detroit
Club and he says What makes you think you are
going to Detroit? I says Comiskey asked wavers
on me and Detroit did not give no wavers. He
says Well that is not no sign that you are going
to Detroit. If Comiskey can't get you out of the
league he will probily keep you himself and it is
a cinch he is not going to give no pitcher to Detroit no matter how rotten he is.

I says What do you mean? And he says You
just stick round town till you hear from Comiskey
and I guess you will hear pretty soon because he
is comeing back from the Coast next Saturday. I
says Well the only thing he can tell me is to

report to Detroit because I won't never pitch
again for the White Sox. Then John gets fresh
and says I suppose you will quit the game and
live on your saveings and then I blowed out of
the office because I was scared I would loose my
temper and break something.

So you see Al what I am up against. I won't
never pitch for the White Sox again and I want
to get with the Detroit Club but how can I if
Comiskey won't let me go? All I can do is stick
round till next Saturday and then I will see
Comiskey and I guess when I tell him what I
think of him he will be glad to let me go to Detroit or anywheres else. I will have something
on him this time because I know that he did not
pay no attention to the rules when he told me I
was sold to Milwaukee and if he tries to slip
something over on me I will tell president Johnson of the league all about it and then you will
see where Comiskey heads in at.

Al old pal that $25.00 you give me at the
station the other day is all shot to peaces and I
must ask you to let me have $25.00 more which
will make $75.00 all together includeing the
$25.00 you sent me before I come home. I hate
to ask you this favor old pal but I know you
have got the money. If I am sold to Detroit I

will get some advance money and pay up all
my dedts incluseive.

If he don't let me go to Detroit I will make
him come across with part of my salery for this
year even if I don't pitch for him because I signed
a contract and was ready to do my end of it and
would of if he had not of been nasty and tried
to slip something over on me. If he refuses to
come across I will hire a attorney at law and he
will get it all. So Al you see you have got a
cinch on getting back what you lone me but I
guess you know that Al without all this talk because you have been my old pal for a good many
years and I have allways treated you square and
tried to make you feel that I and you was equals
and that my success was not going to make me
forget my old friends.

Wherever I pitch this year I will insist on a
salery of 5 or $6000 a year. So you see on my
first pay day I will have enough to pay you up
and settle the rest of my dedts but I am not going
to pay no more rent for this rotten flat because
they tell me if a man don't pay no rent for a
while they will put him out. Let them put me
out. I should not worry but will go and rent
my old room that I had before I met Florrie and
got into all this trouble.

The sooner you can send me that $35.00 the better and then I will owe you $85.00 incluseive and I will write and let you know how I come out with Comiskey.

Your pal,   JACK.

Chicago, Illinois, March 12.

FRIEND AL: I got another big supprise for you and this is it I am going to pitch for the White Sox after all. If Comiskey was not a old man I guess I would of lost my temper and beat him up but I am glad now that I kept my temper and did not loose it because I forced him to make a lot of consessions and now it looks like as though I would have a big year both pitching and money.

He got back to town yesterday morning and showed up to his office in the afternoon and I was there waiting for him. He would not see me for a while but finally I acted like as though I was getting tired of waiting and I guess the secretary got scared that I would beat it out of the office and leave them all in the lerch. Anyway he went in and spoke to Comiskey and then come out and says the boss was ready to see me. When I went into the office where he was at he says Well young man what can I do for you? And I says I want you to give me my release so as I can join the Detroit Club down South and get in shape. Then he says What makes you think you are going to join the Detroit Club? Because we need you here. I says Then why did you try to sell me to Milwaukee? But you could not because you could not get no wavers.

Then he says I thought I was doing you a favor by sending you to Milwaukee because they make a lot of beer up there. I says What do you mean? He says You been keeping in shape all this winter by trying to drink this town dry and besides that you tried to hold me up for more money when you allready had signed a contract allready and so I was going to send you to Milwaukee and learn you something and besides you tried to go with the Federal League but they would not take you because they was scared to.

I don't know where he found out all that stuff at Al and besides he was wrong when he says I was drinking to much because they is not nobody that can drink more than me and not be effected. But I did not say nothing because I was scared I would forget myself and call him some name and he is a old man. Yes I did say something. I says Well I guess you found out that you could not get me out of the league and then he says Don't never think I could not get

you out of the league. If you think I can't send
you to Milwaukee I will prove it to you that I
can. I says You can't because Detroit won't give
no wavers on me. He says Detroit will give
wavers on you quick enough if I ask them.

Then he says Now you can take your choice
you can stay here and pitch for me at the salery
you signed up for and you can cut out the monkey
business and drink water when you are thirsty or
else you can go up to Milwaukee and drownd
yourself in one of them brewrys. Which shall
it be? I says How can you keep me or send me
to Milwaukee when Detroit has allready claimed
my services? He says Detroit has claimed a lot
of things and they have even claimed the pennant but that is not no sign they will win it. He
says And besides you would not want to pitch
for Detroit because then you would not never
have no chance to pitch against Cobb and show
him up.

Well Al when he says that I knowed he appresiated what a pitcher I am even if he did try
to sell me to Milwaukee or he would not of made
that remark about the way I can show Cobb and
Crawford up. So I says Well if you need me
that bad I will pitch for you but I must have a
new contract. He says Oh I guess we can fix

that up O. K. and he steps out in the next room a while and then he comes back with a new contract. And what do you think it was Al? It was a contract for 3 years so you see I am sure of my job here for 3 years and everything is all O. K.

The contract calls for the same salery a year for 3 years that I was going to get before for only 1 year which is $2800.00 a year and then I will get in on the city serious money too and the Detroit Club don't have no city serious and have no chance to get into the World's Serious with the rotten pitching staff they got. So you see Al he fixed me up good and that shows that he must think a hole lot of me or he would of sent me to Detroit or maybe to Milwaukee but I don't see how he could of did that without no wavers.

Well Al I allmost forgot to tell you that he has gave me a ticket to Los Angeles where the 2d team are practicing at now but where the 1st team will be at in about a week. I am leaving to-night and I guess before I go I will go down to president Johnson and tell him that I am fixed up all O. K. and have not got no kick comeing so that president Johnson will not fine Comiskey for not paying no attention to the rules or get him fired out of the league because I guess Comiskey must be all O. K. and good hearted after all.

I won't pay no attention to what he says about me drinking this town dry because he is all wrong in regards to that. He must of been jokeing I guess because nobody but some boob would think he could drink this town dry but at that I guess I can hold more than anybody and not be effected. But I guess I will cut it out for a while at that because I don't want to get them sore at me after the contract they give me.

I will write to you from Los Angeles Al and let you know what the boys says when they see me and I will bet that they will be tickled to death. The rent man was round to-day but I seen him comeing and he did not find me. I am going to leave the furniture that belongs in the flat in the flat and allso the furniture I bought which don't amount to much because it was not no real Sir Cashion walnut and besides I don't want nothing round me to remind me of Florrie because the sooner her and I forget each other the better.

Tell the boys about my good luck Al but it is not no luck neither because it was comeing to me.

Yours truly,   JACK.

Los Angeles, California, March 16.

AL: Here I am back with the White Sox again and it seems to good to be true because just like I told you they are all tickled to death to see me. Kid Gleason is here in charge of the 2d team and when he seen me come into the hotel he jumped up and hit me in the stumach but he acts like that whenever he feels good so I could not get sore at him though he had no right to hit me in the stumach. If he had of did it in ernest I would of walloped him in the jaw.

He says Well if here ain't the old lady killer. He ment Al that I am strong with the girls but I am all threw with them now but he don't know nothing about the troubles I had. He says Are you in shape? And I told him Yes I am. He says Yes you look in shape like a barrel. I says They is not no fat on me and if I am a little bit bigger than last year it is because my mussels is bigger. He says Yes your stumach mussels is emense and you must of gave them plenty of exercise. Wait till Bodie sees you and he will want to stick round you all the time because you make him look like a broom straw or something. I let him kid me along because what is the use of getting mad at him? And besides he is all O. K. even if he is a little rough.

I says to him A little work will fix me up all
O. K. and he says You bet you are going to get
some work because I am going to see to it myself. I says You will have to hurry because you
will be going up to Frisco in a few days and I
am going to stay here and join the 1st club. Then
he says You are not going to do no such a thing.
You are going right along with me. I knowed
he was kidding me then because Callahan would
not never leave me with the 2d team no more
after what I done for him last year and besides
most of the stars generally allways goes with the
1st team on the training trip.

Well I seen all the rest of the boys that is here
with the 2d team and they all acted like as if
they was glad to see me and why should not they
be when they know that me being here with the
White Sox and not with Detroit means that Callahan won't have to do no worrying about his
pitching staff? But they is four or 5 young recrut
pitchers with the team here and I bet they is not
so glad to see me because what chance have they
got?

If I was Comiskey and Callahan I would not
spend no money on new pitchers because with
me and 1 or 2 of the other boys we got the best
pitching staff in the league. And instead of

spending the money for new pitching recruits I would put it all in a lump and buy Ty Cobb or Sam Crawford off of Detroit or somebody else who can hit and Cobb and Crawford is both real hitters Al even if I did make them look like suckers. Who wouldn't?

Well Al to-morrow A. M. I am going out and work a little and in the P. M. I will watch the game between we and the Venice Club but I won't pitch none because Gleason would not dare take no chances of me hurting my arm. I will write to you in a few days from here because no matter what Gleason says I am going to stick here with the 1st team because I know Callahan will want me along with him for a attraction.

Your pal,   JACK.

San Francisco, California, March 20.

FRIEND AL: Well Al here I am back in old Frisco with the 2d team but I will tell you how it happened Al. Yesterday Gleason told me to pack up and get ready to leave Los Angeles with him and I says No I am going to stick here and wait for the 1st team and then he says I guess I must of overlooked something in the papers because I did not see nothing about you being appointed manager of the club. I says No I am not manager but Callahan is manager and he will want to keep me with him. He says I got a wire from Callahan telling me to keep you with my club but of coarse if you know what Callahan wants better than he knows it himself why then go ahead and stay here or go jump in the Pacific Ocean.

Then he says I know why you don't want to go with me and I says Why? And he says Because you know I will make you work and won't let you eat everything on the bill of fair include-ing the name of the hotel at which we are stopping at. That made me sore and I was just going to call him when he says Did not you marry Mrs. Allen's sister? And I says Yes but that is not none of your business. Then he says Well I don't want to butt into your business but I heard you and your wife had some kind of a argument and she beat it. I says Yes she give me a rotten deal. He says Well then I don't see where it is going to be very pleasant for you traveling round with the 1st club because Allen and his wife is both with that club and what do you want to be mixed up with them for? I says I am not scared of Allen or his wife or no other old hen.

So here I am Al with the 2d team but it is only for a while till Callahan gets sick of some

of them pitchers he has got and sends for me so
as he can see some real pitching. And besides
I am glad to be here in Frisco where I made so
many friends when I was pitching here for a short
time till Callahan heard about my work and
called me back to the big show where I belong
at and nowheres else.

Yours truly,   JACK.

San Francisco, California, March 25.

OLD PAL: Al I got a supprise for you. Who
do you think I seen last night? Nobody but
Hazel. Her name now is Hazel Levy because
you know Al she married Kid Levy the middle-
weight and I wish he was champion of the world
Al because then it would not take me more than
about a minute to be champion of the world myself. I have not got nothing against him though
because he married her and if he had not of I
probily would of married her myself but at that
she could not of treated me no worse than Florrie.
Well they was setting at a table in the cafe where
her and I use to go pretty near every night. She
spotted me when I first come in and sends a waiter
over to ask me to come and have a drink with
them. I went over because they was no use being
nasty and let bygones be bygones.

She interduced me to her husband and he asked me what was I drinking. Then she butts in and says Oh you must let Mr. Keefe buy the drinks because it hurts his feelings to have somebody else buy the drinks. Then Levy says Oh he is one of these here spendrifts is he? and she says Yes he don't care no more about a nichol than his right eye does. I says I guess you have got no holler comeing on the way I spend my money. I don't steal no money anyway. She says What do you mean? and I says I guess you know what I mean. How about that $30.00 that you borrowed off of me and never give it back? Then her husband cuts in and says You cut that line of talk out or I will bust you. I says Yes you will. And he says Yes I will.

Well Al what was the use of me starting trouble with him when he has got enough trouble right to home and besides as I say I have not got nothing against him. So I got up and blowed away from the table and I bet he was relieved when he seen I was not going to start nothing. I beat it out of there a while afterward because I was not drinking nothing and I don't have no fun setting round a place and lapping up ginger ail or something. And besides the music was rotten.

Al I am certainly glad I throwed Hazel over

because she has grew to be as big as a horse and is all painted up. I don't care nothing about them big dolls no more or about no other kind neither. I am off of them all. They can all of them die and I should not worry.

Well Al I done my first pitching of the year this P. M. and I guess I showed them that I was in just as good a shape as some of them birds that has been working a month. I worked 4 innings against my old team the San Francisco Club and I give them nothing but fast ones but they sure was fast ones and you could hear them zip. Charlie O'Leary was trying to get out of the way of one of them and it hit his bat and went over first base for a base hit but at that Fournier would of eat it up if it had of been Chase playing first base instead of Fournier.

That was the only hit they got off of me and they ought to of been ashamed to of tooken that one. But Gleason don't appresiate my work and him and I allmost come to blows at supper. I was pretty hungry and I ordered some stake and some eggs and some pie and some ice cream and some coffee and a glass of milk but Gleason would not let me have the pie or the milk and would not let me eat more than ½ the stake. And it is a wonder I did not bust him and tell him to mind his own business. I says What right have you got to tell me what to eat? And he says You don't need nobody to tell you what to eat you need somebody to keep you from floundering yourself. I says Why can't I eat what I want to when I have worked good?

He says Who told you you worked good and I says I did not need nobody to tell me. I know I worked good because they could not do nothing with me. He says Well it is a good thing for you that they did not start bunting because if you had of went to stoop over and pick up the ball you would of busted wide open. I says Why? and he says because you are hog fat and if you don't let up on the stable and fancy groceries we will have to pay 2 fairs to get you back to Chi. I don't remember now what I says to him but I says something you can bet on that. You know me Al.

I wish Al that Callahan would hurry up and order me to join the 1st team. If he don't Al I believe Gleason will starve me to death. A little slob like him don't realize that a big man like I needs good food and plenty of it.

Your pal,   JACK.

Salt Lake City, Utah, April 1.

AL: Well Al we are on our way East and I am still with the 2d team and I don't understand why Callahan don't order me to join the 1st team but maybe it is because he knows that I am all right and have got the stuff and he wants to keep them other guys round where he can see if they have got anything.

The recrut pitchers that is along with our club have not got nothing and the scout that reckommended them must of been full of hops or something. It is not no common thing for a club to pick up a man that has got the stuff to make him a star up here and the White Sox was pretty lucky to land me but I don't understand why they throw their money away on new pitchers when none of them is no good and besides who would want a better pitching staff than we got right now without no raw recruts and bushers.

I worked in Oakland the day before yesterday but he only let me go the 1st 4 innings. I bet them Oakland birds was glad when he took me out. When I was in that league I use to just throw my glove in the box and them Oakland birds was licked and honest Al some of them turned white when they seen I was going to pitch the other day.

I felt kind of sorry for them and I did not give
them all I had so they got 5 or 6 hits and scored
a couple of runs. I was not feeling very good
at that and besides we got some awful excuses
for a ball player on this club and the support
they give me was the rottenest I ever seen gave
anybody. But some of them won't be in this league
more than about 10 minutes more so I should not
fret as they say.

We play here this afternoon and I don't believe I will work because the team they got here
is not worth wasteing nobody on. They must be
a lot of boobs in this town Al because they tell
me that some of them has got ½ a dozen wives
or so. And what a man wants with 1 wife is a
misery to me let alone a ½ dozen.

I will probily work against Denver because
they got a good club and was champions of the
Western League last year. I will make them
think they are champions of the Epworth League
or something.   Yours truly,   Jack.

Des Moines, Iowa, April 10.

Friend Al: We got here this A. M. and this
is our last stop and we will be in old Chi to-
morrow to open the season. The 1st team gets
home to-day and I would be there with them if

Callahan was a real manager who knowed something about manageing because.if I am going to open the season I should ought to have 1 day of rest at home so I would have all my strenth to open the season. The Cleveland Club will be there to open against us and Callahan must know that I have got them licked any time I start against them.

As soon as my name is announced to pitch the Cleveland Club is licked or any other club when I am right and they don't kick the game away behind me.

Gleason told me on the train last night that I was going to pitch here to-day but I bet by this time he has got orders from Callahan to let me rest and to not give me no more work because suppose even if I did not start the game to-morrow I probily will have to finish it.

Gleason has been sticking round me like as if I had a million bucks or something. I can't even sit down and smoke a cigar but what he is there to knock the ashes off of it. He is O. K. and good-hearted if he is a little rough and keeps hitting me in the stumach but I wish he would leave me alone sometimes espesially at meals. He was in to breakfast with me this A. M. and after I got threw I snuck off down the street and got something to eat. That is not right because it costs me money when I have to go away from the hotel and eat and what right has he got to try and help me order my meals? Because he don't know what I want and what my stumach wants.

My stumach don't want to have him punching it all the time but he keeps on doing it. So that shows he don't know what is good for me. But is a old man Al otherwise I would not stand for the stuff he pulls. The 1st thing I am going to do when we get to Chi is I am going to a resturunt somewheres and get a good meal where Gleason or no one else can't get at me. I know allready what I am going to eat and that is a big stake and a apple pie and that is not all.

Well Al watch the papers and you will see what I done to that Cleveland Club and I hope Lajoie and Jackson is both in good shape because I don't want to pick on no cripples.

Your pal,   JACK.

Chicago, Illinois, April 16.
OLD PAL: Yesterday was the 1st pay day old pal and I know I promised to pay you what I owe you and it is $75.00 because when I asked you for $35.00 before I went West you only sent me $25.00 which makes the hole sum $75.00.

Well Al I can't pay you now because the pay we drawed was only for 4 days and did not amount to nothing and I had to buy a meal ticket and fix up about my room rent.

And then they is another thing Al which I will tell you about. I come into the clubhouse the day the season opened and the 1st guy I seen was Allen. I was going up to bust him but he come up and held his hand out and what was they for me to do but shake hands with him if he is going to be yellow like that? He says Well Jack I am glad they did not send you to Milwaukee and I bet you will have a big year. I says Yes I will have a big year O. K. if you don't sick another 1 of your sister-in-laws on to me. He says Oh don't let they be no hard feelings about that. You know it was not no fault of mine and I bet if you was to write to Florrie everything could be fixed up O. K.

I says I don't want to write to no Florrie but I will get a attorney at law to write to her. He says You don't even know where she is at and I says I don't care where she is at. Where is she? He says She is down to her home in Waco, Texas, and if I was you I would write to her myself and not let no attorney at law write to her because that would get her mad and besides what do you

want a attorney at law to write to her about? I
says I am going to sew her for a bill of divorce.

Then he says On what grounds? and I says
Dessertion. He says You better not do no such
thing or she will sew you for a bill of divorce
for none support and then you will look like a
cheap guy. I says I don't care what I look like.
So you see Al I had to send Florrie $10.00 or
maybe she would be mean enough to sew me for
a bill of divorce on the ground of none support
and that would make me look bad.

Well Al, Allen told me his wife wanted to talk
to me and try and fix things up between I and
Florrie but I give him to understand that I would
not stand for no meeting with his wife and he
says Well suit yourself about that but they is no
reason you and I should quarrel.

You see Al he don't want no mix-up with me
because he knows he could not get nothing but
the worst of it. I will be friends with him but
I won't have nothing to do with Marie because
if it had not of been for she and Florrie I would
have money in the bank besides not being in no
danger of getting sewed for none support.

I guess you must of read about Joe Benz getting
married and I guess he must of got a good wife
and 1 that don't bother him all the time because

he pitched the opening game and shut Cleveland out with 2 hits. He was pretty good Al, better than I ever seen him and they was a couple of times when his fast ball was pretty near as fast as mine.

I have not worked yet Al and I asked Callahan to-day what was the matter and he says I was waiting for you to get in shape. I says I am in shape now and I notice that when I was pitching in practice this A. M. they did not hit nothing out of the infield. He says That was because you are so spread out that they could not get nothing past you. He says The way you are now you cover more ground than the grand stand. I says Is that so? And he walked away.

We go out on a trip to Cleveland and Detroit and St. Louis in a few days and maybe I will take my regular turn then because the other pitchers has been getting away lucky because most of the hitters has not got their batting eye as yet but wait till they begin hitting and then it will take a man like I to stop them.

The 1st of May is our next pay day Al and then I will have enough money so as I can send you the $75.00.   Your pal,   JACK.

Detroit, Michigan, April 28.

FRIEND AL: What do you think of a rotten
manager that bawls me out and fines me $50.00
for loosing a 1 to 0 game in 10 innings when it
was my 1st start this season? And no wonder I
was a little wild in the 10th when I had not had
no chance to work and get control. I got a good
notion to quit this rotten club and jump to the
Federals where a man gets some kind of treatment. Callahan says I throwed the game away
on purpose but I did not do no such a thing Al
because when I throwed that ball at Joe Hill's
head I forgot that the bases was full and besides
if Gleason had not of starved me to death the ball
that hit him in the head would of killed him.

And how could a man go to 1st base and the
winning run be forced in if he was dead which
he should ought to of been the lucky left handed
stiff if I had of had my full strenth to put on my
fast one instead of being ½ starved to death and
weak. But I guess I better tell you how it come
off. The papers will get it all wrong like they
generally allways does.

Callahan asked me this A. M. if I thought I was
hard enough to work and I was tickled to death,
because I seen he was going to give me a chance.
I told him Sure I was in good shape and if them

Tigers scored a run off me he could keep me setting on the bench the rest of the summer. So he says All right I am going to start you and if you go good maybe Gleason will let you eat some supper.

Well Al when I begin warming up I happened to look up in the grand stand and who do you think I seen? Nobody but Violet. She smiled when she seen me but I bet she felt more like crying. Well I smiled back at her because she probily would of broke down and made a seen or something if I had not of. They was not nobody warming up for Detroit when I begin warming up but pretty soon I looked over to their bench and Joe Hill Violet's husband was warming up. I says to myself Well here is where I show that bird up if they got nerve enough to start him against me but probily Jennings don't want to waste no real pitcher on this game which he knows we got cinched and we would of had it cinched Al if they had of got a couple of runs or even 1 run for me.

Well, Jennings come passed our bench just like he allways does and tried to pull some of his funny stuff. He says Hello are you still in the league? I says Yes but I come pretty near not being. I came pretty near being with Detroit. I wish you

could of heard Gleason and Callahan laugh when
I pulled that one on him.   He says something
back but it was not no hot comeback like mine.

Well Al if I had of had any work and my regular control I guess I would of pitched a o hit
game because the only time they could touch me
was when I had to ease up to get them over. Cobb
was out of the game and they told me he was
sick but I guess the truth is that he knowed I was
going to pitch.   Crawford got a couple of lucky
scratch hits off of me because I got in the hole
to him and had to let up.   But the way that lucky
left handed Hill got by was something awful and
if I was as lucky as him I would quit pitching
and shoot craps or something.

Our club can't hit nothing anyway.   But batting against this bird was just like hitting fungos.
His curve ball broke about ½ a inch and you
could of wrote your name and address on his fast
one while it was comeing up there.   He had good
control but who would not when they put nothing on the ball?

Well Al we could not get started against the
lucky stiff and they could not do nothing with
me even if my suport was rotten and I give a
couple or 3 or 4 bases on balls but when they was
men waiting to score I zipped them threw there

so as they could not see them let alone hit them. Every time I come to the bench between innings I looked up to where Violet was setting and give her a smile and she smiled back and once I seen her clapping her hands at me after I had made Moriarty pop up in the pinch.

Well we come along to the 10th inning, 0 and 0, and all of a sudden we got after him. Bodie hits one and Schalk gets 2 strikes and 2 balls and then singles. Callahan tells Alcock to bunt and he does it but Hill sprawls all over himself like the big boob he is and the bases is full with nobody down. Well Gleason and Callahan argude about should they send somebody up for me or let me go up there and I says Let me go up there because I can murder this bird and Callahan says Well they is nobody out so go up and take a wallop.

Honest Al if this guy had of had anything at all I would of hit 1 out of the park, but he did not have even a glove. And how can a man hit pitching which is not no pitching at all but just slopping them up? When I went up there I hollered to him and says Stick 1 over here now you yellow stiff. And he says Yes I can stick them over allright and that is where I got something on you.

Well Al I hit a foul off of him that would of

been a fare ball and broke up the game if the
wind had not of been against it. Then I swung
and missed a curve that I don't see how I missed
it. The next 1 was a yard outside and this Evans
calls it a strike. He has had it in for me ever
since last year when he tried to get funny with
me and I says something back to him that stung
him. So he calls this 3d strike on me and I felt
like murdering him. But what is the use?

I throwed down my bat and come back to the
bench and I was glad Callahan and Gleason was
out on the coaching line or they probily would
of said something to me and I would of cut loose
and beat them up. Well Al Weaver and Blackburne looked like a couple of rums up there and
we don't score where we ought to of had 3 or 4
runs with any kind of hitting.

I would of been all O. K. in spite of that peace
of rotten luck if this big Hill had of walked to
the bench and not said nothing like a real pitcher.
But what does he do but wait out there till I
start for the box and I says Get on to the bench
you lucky stiff or do you want me to hand you
something? He says I don't want nothing more
of yourn. I allready got your girl and your goat.

Well Al what do you think of a man that would
say a thing like that? And nobody but a left

hander could of. If I had of had a gun I would
of killed him deader than a doornail or something. He starts for the bench and I hollered at
him Wait till you get up to that plate and then
I am going to bean you.

Honest Al I was so mad I could not see the
plate or nothing. I don't even know who it was
come up to bat 1st but whoever it was I hit him
in the arm and he walks to first base. The next
guy bunts and Chase tries to pull off 1 of them
plays of hisn instead of playing safe and he don't
get nobody. Well I kept getting madder and
madder and I walks Stanage who if I had of been
myself would not foul me.

Callahan has Scotty warming up and Gleason
runs out from the bench and tells me I am threw
but Callahan says Wait a minute he is going to
let Hill hit and this big stiff ought to be able
to get him out of the way and that will give
Scotty a chance to get warm. Gleason says You
better not take a chance because the big busher
is hogwild, and they kept argueing till I got sick
of listening to them and I went back to the box
and got ready to pitch. But when I seen this Hill
up there I forgot all about the ball game and I
cut loose at his bean.

Well Al my control was all O. K. this time and

I catched him square on the fourhead and he
dropped like as if he had been shot. But pretty
soon he gets up and gives me the laugh and runs
to first base. I did not know the game was over
till Weaver come up and pulled me off the field.
But if I had not of been ½ starved to death and
weak so as I could not put all my stuff on the ball
you can bet that Hill never would of ran to first
base and Violet would of been a widow and
probily a lot better off than she is now. At that
I never should ought to of tried to kill a left-
hander by hitting him in the head.

Well Al they jumped all over me in the clubhouse and I had to hold myself back or I would
of gave somebody the beating of their life. Callahan tells me I am fined $50.00 and suspended
without no pay. I asked him What for and he
says They would not be no use in telling you
because you have not got no brains. I says Yes
I have to got some brains and he says Yes but
they is in your stumach. And then he says I
wish we had of sent you to Milwaukee and I
come back at him. I says I wish you had of.

Well Al I guess they is no chance of getting
square treatment on this club and you won't be
supprised if you hear of me jumping to the Fed-

erals where a man is treated like a man and not
like no white slave.

Yours truly,   Jack.

Chicago, Illinois, May 2.

Al: I have got to disappoint you again Al.
When I got up to get my pay yesterday they
held out $150.00 on me. $50.00 of it is what
I was fined for loosing a 1 to 0 10-inning game
in Detroit when I was so weak that I should ought
never to of been sent in there and the $100.00
is the advance money that I drawed last winter
and which I had forgot all about and the club
would of forgot about it to if they was not so
tight fisted.

So you see all I get for 2 weeks' pay is about
$80.00 and I sent $25.00 to Florrie so she can't
come no none support business on me.

I am still suspended Al and not drawing no
pay now and I got a notion to hire a attorney
at law and force them to pay my salary or else
jump to the Federals where a man gets good
treatment.

Allen is still after me to come over to his flat
some night and see his wife and let her talk to
me about Florrie but what do I want to talk

about Florrie for or talk about nothing to a nut
left hander's wife?

The Detroit Club is here and Cobb is playing
because he knows I am suspended but I wish
Callahan would call it off and let me work against
them and I would certainly love to work against
this Joe Hill again and I bet they would be a
different story this time because I been getting
something to eat since we been home and I got
back most of my strenth.

Your old pal,   JACK.

Chicago, Illinois, May 5.

FRIEND AL: Well Al if you been reading the
papers you will know before this letter is received
what I done. Before the Detroit Club come here
Joe Hill had win 4 strate but he has not win no
5 strate or won't neither Al because I put a crimp
in his winning streek just like I knowed I would
do if I got a chance when I was feeling good
and had all my strenth. Callahan asked me yesterday A. M. if I thought I had enough rest and
I says Sure because I did not need no rest in the
1st place. Well, he says, I thought maybe if I
layed you off a few days you would do some
thinking and if you done some thinking once in
a while you would be a better pitcher.

Well anyway I worked and I wish you could of saw them Tigers trying to hit me Cobb and Crawford incluseive.   The 1st time Cobb come up Weaver catched a lucky line drive off of him and the next time I eased up a little and Collins run back and took a fly ball off of the fence. But the other times he come up he looked like a sucker except when he come up in the 8th and then he beat out a bunt but allmost anybody is liable to do that once in a while.

Crawford got a scratch hit between Chase and Blackburne in the 2d inning and in the 4th he was gave a three-base hit by this Evans who should ought to be writeing for the papers instead of trying to umpire.   The ball was 2 feet foul and I bet Crawford will tell you the same thing if you ask him.   But what I done to this Hill was awful.   I give him my curve twice when he was up there in the 3d and he missed it a foot.   Then I come with my fast ball right past his nose and I bet if he had not of ducked it would of drove that big horn of hisn clear up in the press box where them rotten reporters sits and smokes their hops.   Then when he was looking for another fast one I slopped up my slow one and he is still swinging at it yet.

But the best of it was that I practally won

my own game. Bodie and Schalk was on when
I come up in the 5th and Hill hollers to me and
says I guess this is where I shoot one of them
bean balls. I says Go ahead and shoot and if
you hit me in the head and I ever find it out I
will write and tell your wife what happened to
you. You see what I was getting at Al. I was
insinuateing that if he beaned me with his fast
one I would not never know nothing about it if
somebody did not tell me because his fast one is
not fast enough to hurt nobody even if it should
hit them in the head. So I says to him Go ahead
and shoot and if you hit me in the head and I
ever find it out I will write and tell your wife
what happened to you. See, Al?

Of coarse you could not hire me to write to
Violet but I did not mean that part of it in ernest.
Well sure enough he shot at my bean and I ducked
out of the way though if it had of hit me it could
not of did no more than tickle. He takes 2 more
shots and misses me and then Jennings hollers
from the bench What are you doing pitching or
trying to win a cigar? So then Hill sees what
a monkey he is making out of himself and tries
to get one over, but I have him 3 balls and nothing and what I done to that groover was a plenty.
She went over Bush's head like a bullet and got

between Cobb and Veach and goes clear to the fence. Bodie and Schalk scores and I would of scored to if anybody else besides Cobb had of been chaseing the ball. I got 2 bases and Weaver scores me with another wallop.

Say, I wish I could of heard what they said to that baby on the bench. Callahan was tickled to death and he says Maybe I will give you back that $50.00 if you keep that stuff up. I guess I will get that $50.00 back next pay day and if I do Al I will pay you the hole $75.00.

Well Al I beat them 5 to 4 and with good support I would of held them to 1 run but what do I care as long as I beat them? I wish though that Violet could of been there and saw it.

Yours truly,   JACK.

Chicago, Illinois, May 29.

OLD PAL: Well Al I have not wrote to you for a long while but it is not because I have forgot you and to show I have not forgot you I am incloseing the $75.00 which I owe you. It is a money order Al and you can get it cashed by takeing it to Joe Higgins at the P. O.

Since I wrote to you Al I been East with the club and I guess you know what I done in the East. The Athaletics did not have no right to

win that 1 game off of me and I will get them
when they come here the week after next. I
beat Boston and just as good as beat New York
twice because I beat them 1 game all alone and
then saved the other for Eddie Cicotte in the
9th inning and shut out the Washington Club
and would of did the same thing if Johnson had
of been working against me instead of this left
handed stiff Boehling.

Speaking of left handers Allen has been going
rotten and I would not be supprised if they sent
him to Milwaukee or Frisco or somewheres.

But I got bigger news than that for you Al.
Florrie is back and we are liveing together in
the spair room at Allen's flat so I hope they don't
send him to Milwaukee or nowheres else because
it is not costing us nothing for room rent and
this is no more than right after the way the Allens
grafted off of us all last winter.

I bet you will be supprised to know that I and
Florrie has made it up and they is a secret about
it Al which I can't tell you now but maybe next
month I will tell you and then you will be more
supprised than ever. It is about I and Florrie
and somebody else. But that is all I can tell
you now.

We got in this A. M. Al and when I got to my

room they was a slip of paper there telling me to call up a phone number so I called it up and it was Allen's flat and Marie answered the phone. And when I reckonized her voice I was going to hang up the phone but she says Wait a minute somebody wants to talk with you. And then Florrie come to the phone and I was going to hang up the phone again when she pulled this secret on me that I was telling you about.

So it is all fixed up between us Al and I wish I could tell you the secret but that will come later. I have tooken my baggage over to Allen's and I am there now writeing to you while Florrie is asleep. And after a while I am going out and mail this letter and get a glass of beer because I think I have got 1 comeing now on account of this secret. Florrie says she is sorry for the way she treated me and she cried when she seen me. So what is the use of me being nasty Al? And let bygones be bygones.

Your pal,   JACK.

Chicago, Illinois, June 16.

FRIEND AL: Al I beat the Athaletics 2 to 1 to-day but I am writing to you to give you the supprise of your life. Old pal I got a baby and he is a boy and we are going to name him Allen

which Florrie thinks is after his uncle and aunt
Allen but which is after you old pal. And she
can call him Allen but I will call him Al because
I don't never go back on my old pals. The baby
was born over to the hospital and it is going to
cost me a bunch of money but I should not worry.
This is the secret I was going to tell you Al and
I am the happyest man in the world and I bet
you are most as tickled to death to hear about it
as I am.

The baby was born just about the time I was
makeing McInnis look like a sucker in the pinch
but they did not tell me nothing about it till after
the game and then they give me a phone messige
in the clubhouse. I went right over there and
everything was all O. K. Little Al is a homely
little skate but I guess all babys is homely and
don't have no looks till they get older and maybe
he will look like Florrie or I then I won't have
no kick comeing.

Be sure and tell Bertha the good news and
tell her everything has came out all right except
that the rent man is still after me about that
flat I had last winter. And I am still paying the
old man $10.00 a month for that house you got
for me and which has not never done me no good.
But I should not worry about money when I got

a real family. Do you get that Al, a real family?

Well Al I am to happy to do no more writeing to-night but I wanted you to be the 1st to get the news and I would of sent you a telegram only I did not want to scare you.

Your pal,   JACK.

Chicago, Illinois, July 2.

OLD PAL: Well old pal I just come back from St. Louis this A. M. and found things in pretty fare shape. Florrie and the baby is out to Allen's and we will stay there till I can find another place. The Dr. was out to look at the baby this A. M. and the baby was waveing his arm round in the air. And Florrie asked was they something the matter with him that he kept waveing his arm. And the Dr. says No he was just getting his exercise.

Well Al I noticed that he never waved his right arm but kept waveing his left arm and I asked the Dr. why was that. Then the Dr. says I guess he must be left handed. That made me sore and I says I guess you doctors don't know it all. And then I turned round and beat it out of the room.

Well Al it would be just my luck to have him left handed and Florrie should ought to of knew

better than to name him after Allen. I am going
to hire another Dr. and see what he has to say
because they must be some way of fixing babys
so as they won't be left handed. And if nessary I
will cut his left arm off of him. Of coarse I
would not do that Al. But how would I feel if
a boy of mine turned out like Allen and Joe Hill
and some of them other nuts?

We have a game with St. Louis to-morrow and
a double header on the 4th of July. I guess
probily Callahan will work me in one of the 4th
of July games on account of the holiday crowd.

Your pal,   JACK.

P. S.   Maybe I should ought to leave the kid
left handed so as he can have some of their luck.
The lucky stiffs.

5

The Busher's Kid

Chicago, Illinois, July 31.

FRIEND AL: Well Al what do you think of little Al now? But I guess I better tell you first what he done. Maybe you won't believe what I am telling you but did you ever catch me telling you a lie? I guess you know you did not Al. Well we got back from the East this A. M. and I don't have to tell you we had a rotten trip and if it had not of been for me beating Boston once and the Athaletics two times we would of been ashamed to come home.

I guess these here other pitchers thought we was haveing a vacation and when they go up in the office to-morrow to get there checks they should ought to be arrested if they take them. I would not go nowheres near Comiskey if I had not of did better than them others but I can go and get my pay and feel all O. K. about it because I done something to ern it.

Me loseing that game in Washington was a

crime and Callahan says so himself. This here
Weaver throwed it away for me and I would not
be surprised if he done it from spitework because
him and Scott is pals and probily he did not want
to see me winning all them games when Scott
was getting knocked out of the box. And no
wonder when he has not got no stuff. I wish I
knowed for sure that Weaver was throwing me
down and if I knowed for sure I would put him
in a hospital or somewheres.

But I was going to tell you what the kid done
Al. So here goes. We are still liveing at Allen's
and his wife. So I and him come home together
from the train. Well Florrie and Marie was both
up and the baby was up too—that is he was not
up but he was woke up. I beat it right into the
room where he was at and Florrie come in with
me. I says Hello Al and what do you suppose
he done. Well Al he did not say Hello pa or
nothing like that because he is not only one month
old. But he smiled at me just like as if he was
glad to see me and I guess maybe he was at that.

I was tickled to death and I says to Florrie
Did you see that. And she says See what. I says
The baby smiled at me. Then she says They is
something the matter with his stumach. I says
I suppose because a baby smiles that is a sign they

is something the matter with his stumach and if
he had the toothacke he would laugh. She says
You think your smart but I am telling you that
he was not smileing at all but he was makeing a
face because they is something the matter with
his stumach. I says I guess I know the difference
if somebody is smileing or makeing a face. And
she says I guess you don't know nothing about
babys because you never had none before. I says
How many have you had. And then she got sore
and beat it out of the room.

I did not care because I wanted to be in there
alone with him and see would he smile at me
again. And sure enough Al he did. Then I
called Allen in and when the baby seen him he
begin to cry. So you see I was right and Florrie
was wrong. It don't take a man no time at all
to get wise to these babys and it don't take them
long to know if a man is there father or there
uncle.

When he begin to cry I chased Allen out of
the room and called Florrie because she should
ought to know by this time how to make him stop
crying. But she was still sore and she says Let
him cry or if you know so much about babys make
him stop yourself. I says Maybe he is sick. And
she says I was just telling you that he had a pane

in his stumach or he would not of made that face that you said was smileing at you.

I says Do you think we should ought to call the doctor but she says No if you call the doctor every time he has the stumach acke you might just as well tell him he should bring his trunk along and stay here. She says All babys have collect and they is not no use fusing about it but come and get your breakfast.

Well Al I did not injoy my breakfast because the baby was crying all the time and I knowed he probily wanted I should come in and visit with him. So I just eat the prunes and drunk a little coffee and did not wait for the rest of it and sure enough when I went back in our room and started talking to him he started smileing again and pretty soon he went to sleep so you see Al he was smileing and not makeing no face and that was a hole lot of bunk about him haveing the collect. But I don't suppose I should ought to find fault with Florrie for not knowing no better because she has not never had no babys before but still and all I should think she should ought to of learned something about them by this time or ask somebody.

Well Al little Al is woke up again and is crying and I just about got time to fix him up and get him asleep again and then I will have to go to the ball park because we got a poseponed game to play with Detroit and Callahan will probily want me to work though I pitched the next to the last game in New York and would of gave them a good beating except for Schalk dropping that ball at the plate but I got it on these Detroit babys and when my name is announced to pitch they feel like forfiting the game. I won't try for no strike out record because I want them to hit the first ball and get the game over with quick so as I can get back here and take care of little Al.

Your pal,   Jack.

P. S. Babys is great stuff Al and if I was you I would not wait no longer but would hurry up and adopt 1 somewheres.

Chicago, Illinois, August 15.

Old Pal: What do you think Al. Kid Gleason is comeing over to the flat and look at the baby the day after to-morrow when we don't have no game skeduled but we have to practice in the A. M. because we been going so rotten. I had a hard time makeing him promise to come but he is comeing and I bet he will be glad he come when he has came. I says to him in the clubhouse Do

you want to see a real baby? And he says You're
real enough for me Boy.

I says No I am talking about babys. He says
Oh I thought you was talking about ice cream
soda or something. I says No I want you to come
over to the flat to-morrow and take a look at
my kid and tell me what you think of him. He
says I can tell you what I think of him without
takeing no look at him. I think he is out of luck.
I says What do you mean out of luck. But he
just laughed and would not say no more.

I asked him again would he come over to the
flat and look at the baby and he says he had
troubles enough without that and kidded along
for a while but finally he seen I was in ernest
and then he says he would come if I would keep
the missus out of the room while he was there
because he says if she seen him she would probily
be sorry she married me.

He was just jokeing and I did not take no
excepshun to his remarks because Florrie could
not never fall for him after seeing me because
he is not no big stropping man like I am but a
little runt and look at how old he is. But I am
glad he is comeing because he will think more of
me when he sees what a fine baby I got though
he thinks a hole lot of me now because look what

I done for the club and where would they be at
if I had jumped to the Federal like I once thought
I would. I will tell you what he says about little
Al and I bet he will say he never seen no prettyer
baby but even if he don't say nothing at all I
will know he is kidding.

The Boston Club comes here to-morrow and
plays 4 days includeing the day after to-morrow
when they is not no game. So on account of the
off day maybe I will work twice against them and
if I do they will wish the grounds had of burned
down.   Yours truly,   JACK.

Chicago, Illinois, August 17.

AL: Well old pal what did I tell you about
what I would do to that Boston Club? And now
Al I have beat every club in the league this year
because yesterday was the first time I beat the
Boston Club this year but now I have beat all
of them and most of them severel times.

This should ought to of gave me a record of
16 wins and o defeats because the only games I
lost was throwed away behind me but instead of
that my record is 10 games win and 6 defeats and
that don't include the games I finished up and
helped the other boys win which is about 6 more
alltogether but what do I care about my record

Al? because I am not the kind of man that is allways thinking about there record and playing for there record while I am satisfied if I give the club the best I got and if I win all O. K. And if I lose who's fault is it. Not mine Al.

I asked Callahan would he let me work against the Boston Club again before they go away and he says I guess I will have to because you are going better than anybody else on the club. So you see Al he is beginning to appresiate my work and from now on I will pitch in my regular turn and a hole lot offtener then that and probily Comiskey will see the stuff I am made from and will raise my salery next year even if he has got me signed for 3 years and for the same salery I am getting now.

But all that is not what I was going to tell you Al and what I was going to tell you was about Gleason comeing to see the baby and what he thought about him. I sent Florrie and Marie downtown and says I would take care of little Al and they was glad to go because Florrie says she should ought to buy some new shoes though I don't see what she wants of no new shoes when she is going to be tied up in the flat for a long time yet on account of the baby and nobody cares if she wears shoes in the flat or goes round in her bear feet. But I was glad to get rid of the both of them for a while because little Al acts better when they is not no women round and you can't blame him.

The baby was woke up when Gleason come in and I and him went right in the room where he was laying. Gleason takes a look at him and says Well that is a mighty fine baby and you must of boughten him. I says What do you mean? And he says I don't believe he is your own baby because he looks humaner than most babys. And I says Why should not he look human. And he says Why should he.

Then he goes to work and picks the baby right up and I was a-scared he would drop him because even I have not never picked him up though I am his father and would be a-scared of hurting him. I says Here, don't pick him up and he says Why not? He says Are you going to leave him on that there bed the rest of his life? I says No but you don't know how to handle him. He says I have handled a hole lot bigger babys than him or else Callahan would not keep me.

Then he starts patting the baby's head and I says Here, don't do that because he has got a soft spot in his head and you might hit it. He says I thought he was your baby and I says Well

he is my baby and he says Well then they can't
be no soft spot in his head.   Then he lays little
Al down because he seen I was in ernest and as
soon as he lays him down the baby begins to cry.
Then Gleason says See he don't want me to lay
him down and I says Maybe he has got a pane in
his stumach and he says I would not be supprised
because he just took a good look at his father.

But little Al did not act like as if he had a
pane in his stumach and he kept sticking his finger
in his mouth and crying.   And Gleason says He
acts like as if he had a toothacke.   I says How
could he have a toothacke when he has not got
no teeth?   He says That is easy.   I have saw a
lot of pitchers complane that there arm was sore
when they did not have no arm.

Then he asked me what was the baby's name
and I told him Allen but that he was not named
after my brother-in-law Allen.   And Gleason says
I should hope not.   I should hope you would have
better sense then to name him after a left hander.
So you see Al he don't like them no better then
I do even if he does jolly Allen and Russell along
and make them think they can pitch.

Pretty soon he says What are you going to
make out of him, a ball player?   I says Yes I am
going to make a hitter out of him so as he can

join the White Sox and then maybe they will get a couple of runs once in a while. He says If I was you I would let him pitch and then you won't have to give him no educasion. Besides, he says, he looks now like he would divellop into a grate spitter.

Well I happened to look out of the window and seen Florrie and Marie comeing acrost Indiana Avenue and I told Gleason about it. And you ought to of seen him run. I asked him what was his hurry and he says it was in his contract that he was not to talk to no women but I knowed he was kidding because I allready seen him talking to severel of the players' wifes when they was on trips with us and they acted like as if they thought he was a regular comeedion though they really is not nothing funny about what he says only it is easy to make women laugh when they have not got no grouch on about something.

Well Al I am glad Gleason has saw the baby and maybe he will fix it with Callahan so as I won't have to go to morning practice every A. M. because I should ought to be home takeing care of little Al when Florrie is washing the dishs or helping Marie round the house. And besides why should I wear myself all out in practice because I don't need to practice pitching and I could hit

as well as the rest of the men on our club if I
never seen no practice.

After we get threw with Boston, Washington
comes here and then we go to St. Louis and Cleveland and then come home and then go East again.
And after that we are pretty near threw except the
city serious. Callahan is not going to work me
no more after I beat Boston again till it is this
here Johnson's turn to pitch for Washington. And
I hope it is not his turn to work the 1st game of
the serious because then I would not have no rest
between the last game against Boston and the 1st
game against Washington.

But rest or no rest I will work against this
here Johnson and show him up for giveing me
that trimming in Washington, the lucky stiff. I
wish I had a team like the Athaletics behind me
and I would loose about 1 game every 6 years
and then they would have to get all the best of
it from these rotten umpires.

Your pal,   JACK.

New York, New York, September 16.

FRIEND AL: Al it is not no fun running round
the country no more and I wish this dam trip
was over so as I could go home and see how little
Al is getting along because Florrie has not wrote

since we was in Philly which was the first stop
on this trip. I am a-scared they is something the
matter with the little fellow or else she would of
wrote but then if they was something the matter
with him she would of sent me a telegram or
something and let me know.

So I guess they can't be nothing the matter
with him. Still and all I don't see why she has
not wrote when she knows or should ought to
know that I would be worrying about the baby.
If I don't get no letter to-morrow I am going to
send her a telegram and ask her what is the matter with him because I am positive she would of
wrote if they was not something the matter with
him.

The boys has been trying to get me to go out
nights and see a show or something but I have
not got no heart to go to shows. And besides
Callahan has not gave us no pass to no show
on this trip. I guess probily he is sore on account
of the rotten way the club has been going but
still he should ought not to be sore on me because
I have win 3 out of my last 4 games and would
of win the other if he had not of started me
against them with only 1 day's rest and the Athaletics at that, who a man should ought not to
pitch against if he don't feel good.

I asked Allen if he had heard from Marie and he says Yes he did but she did not say nothing about little Al except that he was keeping her awake nights balling. So maybe Al if little Al is balling they is something wrong with him. I am going to send Florrie a telegram to-morrow —that is if I don't get no letter.

If they is something the matter with him I will ask Callahan to send me home and he won't want to do it neither because who else has he got that is a regular winner. But if little Al is sick and Callahan won't let me go home I will go home anyway. You know me Al.

Yours truly,   JACK.

Boston, Massachusetts, September 24.

AL: I bet if Florrie was a man she would be a left hander. What do you think she done now Al? I sent her a telegram from New York when I did not get no letter from her and she did not pay no atension to the telegram. Then when we got up here I sent her another telegram and it was not more then five minutes after I sent the 2d telegram till I got a letter from her. And it said the baby was all O. K. but she had been so busy takeing care of him that she had not had no time to write.

Well when I got the letter I chased out to see if I could catch the boy who had took my telegram but he had went allready so I was spending $.60 for nothing. Then what does Florrie do but send me a telegram after she got my second telegram and tell me that little Al is all O. K., which I knowed all about then because I had just got her letter. And she sent her telegram c. o. d. and I had to pay for it at this end because she had not paid for it and that was $.60 more but I bet if I had of knew what was in the telegram before I read it I would of told the boy to keep it and would not of gave him no $.60 but how did I know if little Al might not of tooken sick after Florrie had wrote the letter?

I am going to write and ask her if she is trying to send us both to the Poor House or somewheres with her telegrams. I don't care nothing about the $.60 but I like to see a woman use a little judgement though I guess that is impossable.

It is my turn to work to-day and to-night we start West but we have got to stop off at Cleveland on the way. I have got a nosion to ask Callahan to let me go right on threw to Chi if I win to-day and not stop off at no Cleveland but I guess they would not be no use because I have got that Cleveland Club licked the minute I put on

my glove. So probily Callahan will want me
with him though it don't make no difference if
we win or lose now because we have not got no
chance for the pennant. One man can't win no
pennant Al I don't care who he is.

Your pal,   JACK.

Chicago, Illinois, October 2.

FRIEND AL: Well old pal I am all threw till
the city serious and it is all fixed up that I am
going to open the serious and pitch 3 of the games
if nessary. The club has went to Detroit to wind
up the season and Callahan did not take me along
but left me here with a couple other pitchers and
Billy Sullivan and told me all as I would have
to do was go over to the park the next 3 days and
warm up a little so as to keep in shape. But I
don't need to be in no shape to beat them Cubs
Al. But it is a good thing Al that Allen was
tooken on the trip to Detroit or I guess I would
of killed him. He has not been going good and
he has been acting and talking nasty to everybody because he can't win no games.

Well the 1st night we was home after the trip
little Al was haveing a bad night and was balling
pretty hard and they could not nobody in the
flat get no sleep. Florrie says he was haveing

the collect and I says Why should he have the collect all the time when he did not drink nothing but milk? She says she guessed the milk did not agree with him and upsetted his stumach. I says Well he must take after his mother if his stumach gets upsetted every time he takes a drink because if he took after his father he could drink a hole lot and not never be effected. She says You should ought to remember he has only got a little stumach and not a great big resservoire. I says Well if the milk don't agree with him why don't you give him something else? She says Yes I suppose I should ought to give him weeny worst or something.

Allen must of heard us talking because he hollered something and I did not hear what it was so I told him to say it over and he says Give the little X-eyed brat poison and we would all be better off. I says You better take poison yourself because maybe a rotten pitcher like you could get by in the league where you're going when you die. Then I says Besides I would rather my baby was X-eyed then to have him left handed. He says It is better for him that he is X-eyed or else he might get a good look at you and then he would shoot himself. I says Is that so? and he shut up. Little Al is not no more X-eyed than

you or I are Al and that was what made me sore
because what right did Allen have to talk like
that when he knowed he was lying?

Well the next morning Allen nor I did not
speak to each other and I seen he was sorry for
the way he had talked and I was willing to fix
things up because what is the use of staying sore
at a man that don't know no better.

But all of a sudden he says When are you
going to pay me what you owe me? I says What
do you mean? And he says You been liveing here
all summer and I been paying all the bills. I
says Did not you and Marie ask us to come here
and stay with you and it would not cost us nothing. He says Yes but we did not mean it was a
life sentence. You are getting more money than
me and you don't never spend a nichol. All I
have to do is pay the rent and buy your food and
it would take a millionare or something to feed
you.

Then he says I would not make no holler about
you grafting off of me if that brat would shut
up nights and give somebody a chance to sleep.
I says You should ought to get all the sleep you
need on the bench. Besides, I says, who done
the grafting all last winter and without no invatation? If he had of said another word I was

going to bust him but just then Marie come in and he shut up.

The more I thought about what he said and him a rotten left hander that should ought to be hussling freiht the more madder I got and if he had of opened his head to me the last day or 2 before he went to Detroit I guess I would of finished him. But Marie stuck pretty close to the both of us when we was together and I guess she knowed they was something in the air and did not want to see her husband get the worst of it though if he was my husband and I was a woman I would push him under a st. car.

But Al I won't even stand for him saying that I am grafting off of him and I and Florrie will get away from here and get a flat of our own as soon as the city serious is over. I would like to bring her and the kid down to Bedford for the winter but she wont listen to that.

I allmost forgot Al to tell you to be sure and thank Bertha for the little dress she made for little Al. I don't know if it will fit him or not because Florrie has not yet tried it on him yet and she says she is going to use it for a dishrag but I guess she is just kidding.

I suppose you seen where Callahan took me out of that game down to Cleveland but it was not

because I was not going good Al but it was because Callahan seen he was makeing a mistake
wasteing me on that bunch who allmost any
pitcher could beat. They beat us that game at
that but only by one run and it was not no fault
of mine because I was tooken out before they got
the run that give them the game.

Your old pal,   JACK.

Chicago, Illinois, October 4.

FRIEND AL: Well Al the club winds up the
season at Detroit to-morrow and the serious starts
the day after to-morrow and I will be in there
giveing them a battle. I wish I did not have nobody but the Cubs to pitch against all season and
you bet I would have a record that would make
Johnson and Mathewson and some of them other
swell heads look like a dirty doose.

I and Florrie and Marie has been haveing a
argument about how could Florrie go and see the
city serious games when they is not nobody here
that can take care of the baby because Marie
wants to go and see the games to even though
they is not no more chance of Callahan starting
Allen than a rabbit or something.

Florrie and Marie says I should ought to hire
a nurse to take care of little Al and Florrie got

pretty sore when I told her nothing doing because in the first place I can't afford to pay no nurse a salery and in the second place I would not trust no nurse to take care of the baby because how do I know the nurse is not nothing but a grafter or a dope fiend maybe and should ought not to be left with the baby?

Of coarse Florrie wants to see me pitch and a man can't blame her for that but I won't leave my baby with no nurse Al and Florrie will have to stay home and I will tell her what I done when I get there. I might of gave my consent to haveing a nurse at that if it had not of been for the baby getting so sick last night when I was takeing care of him while Florrie and Marie and Allen was out to a show and if I had not of been home they is no telling what would of happened. It is a cinch that none of them bonehead nurses would of knew what to do.

Allen must of been out of his head because right after supper he says he would take the 2 girls to a show. I says All right go on and I will take care of the baby. Then Florrie says Do you think you can take care of him all O. K.? And I says Have not I tooken care of him before allready? Well, she says, I will leave him with you only don't run in to him every time he cries.

I says Why not? And she says Because it is good
for him to cry. I says You have not got no heart
or you would not talk that way.

They all give me the laugh but I let them get
away with it because I am not picking no fights
with girls and why should I bust this Allen when
he don't know no better and has not got no baby
himself. And I did not want to do nothing that
would stop him takeing the girls to a show because it is time he spent a peace of money on
somebody.

Well they all went out and I went in on the
bed and played with the baby. I wish you could
of saw him Al because he is old enough now to
do stunts and he smiled up at me and waved his
arms and legs round and made a noise like as if
he was trying to say Pa. I did not think Florrie
had gave him enough covers so I rapped him up
in some more and took a blanket off of the big
bed and stuck it round him so as he could not kick
his feet out and catch cold.

I thought once or twice he was going off to
sleep but all of a sudden he begin to cry and I
seen they was something wrong with him. I gave
him some hot water but that made him cry again
and I thought maybe he was to cold yet so I took
another blanket off of Allen's bed and wrapped

that round him but he kept on crying and trying
to kick inside the blankets. And I seen then that
he must have collect or something.

So pretty soon I went to the phone and called
up our regular Dr. and it took him pretty near a
hour to get there and the baby balling all the
time. And when he come he says they was nothing the matter except that the baby was to hot
and told me to take all them blankets off of him
and then soaked me 2 dollars. I had a nosion to
bust his jaw. Well pretty soon he beat it and
then little Al begin crying again and kept getting
worse and worse so finally I got a-scared and run
down to the corner where another Dr. is at and I
brung him up to see what was the matter but he
said he could not see nothing the matter but he
did not charge me a cent so I thought he was not
no robber like our regular doctor even if he was
just as much of a boob.

The baby did not cry none while he was there
but the minute he had went he started crying and
balling again and I seen they was not no use of
fooling no longer so I looked around the house
and found the medicine the doctor left for Allen
when he had a stumach acke once and I give the
baby a little of it in a spoon but I guess he did
not like the taste because he hollered like a Indian

and finally I could not stand it no longer so I
called that second Dr. back again and this time
he seen that the baby was sick and asked me what
I had gave it and I told him some stumach medicine and he says I was a fool and should ought not
to of gave the baby nothing. But while he was
talking the baby stopped crying and went off to
sleep so you see what I done for him was the right
thing to do and them doctors was both off of there
nut.

This second Dr. soaked me 2 dollars the 2d
time though he had not did no more than when he
was there the 1st time and charged me nothing
but they is all a bunch of robbers Al and I would
just as leave trust a policeman.

Right after the baby went to sleep Florrie and
Marie and Allen come home and I told Florrie
what had came off but instead of giveing me credit
she says If you want to kill him why don't
you take a ax? Then Allen butts in and says
Why don't you take a ball and throw it at him?
Then I got sore and I says Well if I did hit him
with a ball I would kill him while if you was
to throw that fast ball of yours at him and hit
him in the head he would think the musketoes
was biteing him and brush them off. But at that,

I says, you could not hit him with a ball except you was aiming at something else.

I guess they was no comeback to that so him and Marie went to there room. Allen should ought to know better than to try and get the best of me by this time and I would shut up anyway if I was him after getting sent home from Detroit with some of the rest of them when he only worked 3 innings up there and they had to take him out or play the rest of the game by electrick lights.

I wish you could be here for the serious Al but you would have to stay at a hotel because we have not got no spair room and it would cost you a hole lot of money. But you can watch the papers and you will see what I done.

Yours truly,   JACK.

Chicago, Illinois, October 6.

DEAR OLD PAL: Probily before you get this letter you will of saw by the paper that we was licked in the first game and that I was tooken out but the papers don't know what really come off so I am going to tell you and you can see for yourself if it was my fault.

I did not never have no more stuff in my life then when I was warming up and I seen the Cubs looking over to our bench and shakeing there heads like they knowed they did not have no chance. O'Day was going to start Cheney who is there best bet and had him warming up but when he seen the smoke I had when I and Schalk was warming up he changed his mind because what was the use of useing his best pitcher when I had all that stuff and it was a cinch that no club in the world could score a run off of me when I had all that stuff?

So he told a couple others to warm up to and when my name was announced to pitch Cheney went and set on the bench and this here left-hander Pierce was announced for them.

Well Al you will see by the paper where I sent there 1st 3 batters back to the bench to get a drink of water and all 3 of them good hitters Leach and Good and this here Saier that hits a hole lot of home runs but would not never hit one off of me if I was O. K. Well we scored a couple in our half and the boys on the bench all says Now you got enough to win easy because they won't never score none off of you.

And they was right to because what chance did they have if this thing that I am going to tell you about had not of happened? We goes along seven innings and only 2 of there men

had got to 1st base one of them on a bad peg of
Weaver's and the other one I walked because this
blind Evans don't know a ball from a strike. We
had not did no more scoreing off of Pierce not
because he had no stuff but because our club could
not take a ball in there hands and hit it out of the
infield.

Well Al I did not tell you that before I come
out to the park I kissed little Al and Florrie good
by and Marie says she was going to stay home
to and keep Florrie Co. and they was not no
reason for Marie to come to the game anyway
because they was not a chance in the world for
Allen to do nothing but hit fungos. Well while
I was doing all this here swell pitching and makeing them Cubs look like a lot of rummys I was
thinking about little Al and Florrie and how glad
they would be when I come home and told them
what I done though of coarse little Al is not only
a little over 3 months of age and how could he
appresiate what I done? But Florrie would.

Well Al when I come in to the bench after there
½ of the 7th I happened to look up to the press
box to see if the reporters had gave Schulte a
hit on that one Weaver throwed away and who
do you think I seen in a box right alongside of
the press box? It was Florrie and Marie and

both of them claping there hands and hollering with the rest of the bugs.

Well old pal I was never so supprised in my life and it just took all the heart out of me. What was they doing there and what had they did with the baby? How did I know that little Al was not sick or maybe dead and balling his head off and nobody round to hear him?

I tried to catch Florrie's eyes but she would not look at me. I hollered her name and the bugs looked at me like as if I was crazy and I was to Al. Well I seen they was not no use of standing out there in front of the stand so I come into the bench and Allen was setting there and I says Did you know your wife and Florrie was up there in the stand? He says No and I says What are they doing here? And he says What would they be doing here—mending there stockings? I felt like busting him and I guess he seen I was mad because he got up off of the bench and beat it down to the corner of the field where some of the others was getting warmed up though why should they have anybody warming up when I was going so good?

Well Al I made up my mind that ball game or no ball game I was not going to have little Al left alone no longer and I seen they was not no

use of sending word to Florrie to go home because they was a big crowd and it would take
maybe 15 or 20 minutes for somebody to get up
to where she was at. So I says to Callahan You
have got to take me out. He says What is the
matter? Is your arm gone? I says No my arm
is not gone but my baby is sick and home all alone.
He says Where is your wife? And I says She
is setting up there in the stand.

Then he says How do you know your baby is
sick? And I says I don't know if he is sick or
not but he is left home all alone. He says Why
don't you send your wife home? And I says I
could not get word to her in time. He says Well
you have only got two innings to go and the way
your going the game will be over in 10 minutes.
I says Yes and before 10 minutes is up my baby
might die and are you going to take me out or
not? He says Get in there and pitch you yellow
dog and if you don't I will take your share of
the serious money away from you.

By this time our part of the inning was over
and I had to go out there and pitch some more
because he would not take me out and he has
not got no heart Al. Well Al how could I pitch
when I kept thinking maybe the baby was dying
right now and maybe if I was home I could do

something? And instead of paying attension to
what I was doing I was thinking about little Al
and looking up there to where Florrie and Marie
was setting and before I knowed what come off
they had the bases full and Callahan took me out.
Well Al I run to the clubhouse and changed
my cloths and beat it for home and I did not even
hear what Callahan and Gleason says to me when
I went by them but I found out after the game
that Scott went in and finished up and they batted
him pretty hard and we was licked 3 and 2.

When I got home the baby was crying but he
was not all alone after all Al because they was
a little girl about 14 years of age there watching
him and Florrie had hired her to take care of him
so as her and Marie could go and see the game.
But just think Al of leaveing little Al with a girl
14 years of age that did not never have no babys
of her own! And what did she know about takeing care of him? Nothing Al.

You should ought to of heard me ball Florrie
out when she got home and I bet she cried pretty
near enough to flood the basemunt. We had it
hot and heavy and the Allens butted in but I soon
showed them where they was at and made them
shut there mouth.

I had a good nosion to go out and get a hole

lot of drinks and was just going to put on my hat when the doorbell rung and there was Kid Gleason. I thought he would be sore and probily try to ball me out and I was not going to stand for nothing but instead of balling me out he come and shook hands with me and interduced himself to Florrie and asked how was little Al.

Well we all set down and Gleason says the club was depending on me to win the serious because I was in the best shape of all the pitchers. And besides the Cubs could not never hit me when I was right and he was telling the truth to.

So he asked me if I would stand for the club hireing a train nurse to stay with the baby the rest of the serious so as Florrie could go and see her husband win the serious but I says No I would not stand for that and Florrie's place was with the baby.

So Gleason and Florrie goes out in the other room and talks a while and I guess he was persuadeing her to stay home because pretty soon they come back in the room and says it was all fixed up and I would not have to worry about little Al the rest of the serious but could give the club the best I got. Gleason just left here a little while ago and I won't work to-morrow Al but I will work the day after and you will see

what I can do when I don't have nothing to worry
me.   Your pal,   JACK.

Chicago, Illinois, October 8.

OLD PAL: Well old pal we got them 2 games
to one now and the serious is sure to be over in
three more days because I can pitch 2 games in
that time if nessary. I shut them out to-day and
they should ought not to of had four hits but
should ought to of had only 2 but Bodie don't
cover no ground and 2 fly balls that he should
ought to of eat up fell safe.

But I beat them anyway and Benz beat them
yesterday but why should he not beat them when
the club made 6 runs for him? All they made
for me was three but all I needed was one because they could not hit me with a shuvvel. When
I come to the bench after the 5th inning they was
a note there for me from the boy that answers
the phone at the ball park and it says that somebody just called up from the flat and says the
baby was asleep and getting along fine. So I felt
good Al and I was better then ever in the 6th.

When I got home Florrie and Marie was both
there and asked me how did the game come out
because I beat Allen home and I told them all
about what I done and I bet Florrie was proud

of me but I supose Marie is a little jellus because how could she help it when Callahan is depending on me to win the serious and her husband is wearing out the wood on the bench? But why should she be sore when it is me that is winning the serious for them? And if it was not for me Allen and all the rest of them would get about $500.00 apeace instead of the winners' share which is about $750.00 apeace.

Cicotte is going to work to-morrow and if he is lucky maybe he can get away with the game and that will leave me to finish up the day after to-morrow but if nessary I can go in to-morrow when they get to hitting Cicotte and stop them and then come back the following day and beat them again. Where would this club be at Al if I had of jumped to the Federal?

Yours truly,   JACK.

Chicago, Illinois, October 11.
FRIEND AL: We done it again Al and I guess the Cubs won't never want to play us again not so long as I am with the club. Before you get this letter you will know what we done and who done it but probily you could of guessed that Al without seeing no paper.

I got 2 more of them phone messiges about the

baby dureing the game and I guess that was what
made me so good because I knowed then that
Florrie was takeing care of him but I could not
help feeling sorry for Florrie because she is a bug
herself and it must of been pretty hard for her to
stay away from the game espesially when she
knowed I was going to pitch and she has been
pretty good to sacrifice her own plesure for little Al.

Cicotte was knocked out of the box the day
before yesterday and then they give this here
Faber a good beating but I wish you could of
saw what they done to Allen when Callahan sent
him in after the game was gone allready. Honest
Al if he had not of been my brother in law I
would of felt like laughing at him because it
looked like as if they would have to call the fire
department to put the side out. They had Bodie
and Collins hollering for help and with there
tongue hanging out from running back to the
fence.

Anyway the serious is all over and I won't have
nothing to do but stay home and play with little
Al but I don't know yet where my home is going
to be at because it is a cinch I won't stay with
Allen no longer. He has not came home since
the game and I suppose he is out somewheres

lapping up some beer and spending some of the winner's share of the money which he would not of had no chance to get in on if it had not of been for me.

I will write and let you know my plans for the winter and I wish Florrie would agree to come to Bedford but nothing doing Al and after her staying home and takeing care of the baby instead of watching me pitch I can't be too hard on her but must leave her have her own way about something.   Your pal,   JACK.

Chicago, Illinois, October 13.

AL: I am all threw with Florrie Al and I bet when you hear about it you won't say it was not no fault of mine but no man liveing who is any kind of a man would act different from how I am acting if he had of been decieved like I been.

Al Florrie and Marie was out to all them games and was not home takeing care of the baby at all and it is not her fault that little Al is not dead and that he was not killed by the nurse they hired to take care of him while they went to the games when I thought they was home takeing care of the baby. And all them phone messiges was just fakes and maybe the baby was sick all the time I was winning them games and balling his head off instead of being asleep like they said he was.

Allen did not never come home at all the night before last and when he come in yesterday he was a sight and I says to him Where have you been? And he says I have been down to the Y. M. C. A. but that is not none of your business. I says Yes you look like as if you had been to the Y. M. C. A. and I know where you have been and you have been out lushing beer. And he says Suppose I have and what are you going to do about it? And I says Nothing but you should ought to be ashamed of yourself and leaveing Marie here while you was out lapping up beer.

Then he says Did you not leave Florrie home while you was getting away with them games, you lucky stiff? And I says Yes but Florrie had to stay home and take care of the baby but Marie don't never have to stay home because where is your baby? You have not got no baby. He says I would not want no X-eyed baby like yourn. Then he says So you think Florrie stayed to home and took care of the baby do you? And I says What do you mean? And he says You better ask her.

So when Florrie come in and heard us talking she busted out crying and then I found out what they put over on me. It is a wonder Al that I did not take some of that cheap furniture them Allens got and bust it over there heads, Allen and Florrie. This is what they done Al. The club give Florrie $50.00 to stay home and take care of the baby and she said she would and she was to call up every so often and tell me the baby was all O. K. But this here Marie told her she was a sucker so she hired a nurse for part of the $50.00 and then her and Marie went to the games and beat it out quick after the games was over and come home in a taxicab and chased the nurse out before I got home.

Well Al when I found out what they done I grabbed my hat and goes out and got some drinks and I was so mad I did not know where I was at or what come off and I did not get home till this A. M. And they was all asleep and I been asleep all day and when I woke up Marie and Allen was out but Florrie and I have not spoke to each other and I won't never speak to her again.

But I know now what I am going to do Al and I am going to take little Al and beat it out of here and she can sew me for a bill of divorce and I should not worry because I will have little Al and I will see that he is tooken care of because I guess I can hire a nurse as well as they can and I will pick out a train nurse that knows something.

Maybe I and him and the nurse will come to
Bedford Al but I don't know yet and I will write
and tell you as soon as I make up my mind. Did
you ever hear of a man getting a rottener deal
Al? And after what I done in the serious too.

Your pal,   JACK.

Chicago, Illinois, October 17.

OLD PAL: I and Florrie has made it up Al but
we are threw with Marie and Allen and I and
Florrie and the baby is staying at a hotel here
on Cottage Grove Avenue the same hotel we was
at when we got married only of coarse they was
only the 2 of us then.

And now Al I want to ask you a favor and that
is for you to go and see old man Cutting and tell
him I want to ree-new the lease on that house for
another year because I and Florrie has decided
to spend the winter in Bedford and she will want
to stay there and take care of little Al while I
am away on trips next summer and not stay in
no high-price flat up here. And may be you and
Bertha can help her round the house when I am
not there.

I will tell you how we come to fix things up
Al and you will see that I made her apollojize
to me and after this she will do what I tell her

to and won't never try to put nothing over. We was eating breakfast—I and Florrie and Marie. Allen was still asleep yet because I guess he must of had a bad night and he was snoreing so as you could hear him in the next st. I was not saying nothing to nobody but pretty soon Florrie says to Marie I don't think you and Allen should ought to kick on the baby crying when Allen's snoreing makes more noise than a hole wagonlode of babys. And Marie got sore and says I guess a man has got a right to snore in his own house and you and Jack has been grafting off of us long enough.

Then Florrie says What did Allen do to help win the serious and get that $750.00? Nothing but set on the bench except when they was makeing him look like a sucker the 1 inning he pitched. The trouble with you and Allen is you are jellous of what Jack has did and you know he will be a star up here in the big league when Allen is tending bar which is what he should ought to be doing because then he could get stewed for nothing.

Marie says Take your brat and get out of the house. And Florrie says Don't you worry because we would not stay here no longer if you hired us. So Florrie went in her room and I followed her in and she says Let's pack up and get out.

Then I says Yes but we won't go nowheres

together after what you done to me but you can
go where you dam please and I and little Al will
go to Bedford. Then she says You can't take the
baby because he is mine and if you was to take
him I would have you arrested for kidnaping.
Besides, she says, what would you feed him and
who would take care of him?

I says I would find somebody to take care of
him and I would get him food from a resturunt.
She says He can't eat nothing but milk and I says
Well he has the collect all the time when he is
eating milk and he would not be no worse off if
he was eating watermelon. Well, she says, if
you take him I will have you arrested and sew
you for a bill of divorce for dessertion.

Then she says Jack you should not ought to
find no fault with me for going to them games
because when a woman has a husband that can
pitch like you can do you think she wants to stay
home and not see her husband pitch when a lot of
other women is cheering him and makeing her
feel proud because she is his wife?

Well Al as I said right along it was pretty hard
on Florrie to have to stay home and I could not
hardly blame her for wanting to be out there
where she could see what I done so what was the
use of argueing?

So I told her I would think it over and then I went out and I went and seen a attorney at law and asked him could I take little Al away and he says No I did not have no right to take him away from his mother and besides it would probily kill him to be tooken away from her and then he soaked me $10.00 the robber.

Then I went back and told Florrie I would give her another chance and then her and I packed up and took little Al in a taxicab over to this hotel. We are threw with the Allens Al and let me know right away if I can get that lease for another year because Florrie has gave up and will go to Bedford or anywheres else with me now.

Yours truly,   JACK.

Chicago, Illinois, October 20.

FRIEND AL: Old pal I won't never forget your kindnus and this is to tell you that I and Florrie except your kind invatation to come and stay with you till we can find a house and I guess you won't regret it none because Florrie will livun things up for Bertha and Bertha will be crazy about the baby because you should ought to see how cute he is now Al and not yet four months old. But I bet he will be talking before we know it.

We are comeing on the train that leaves here
at noon Saturday Al and the train leaves here
about 12 o'clock and I don't know what time it
gets to Bedford but it leaves here at noon so we
shall be there probily in time for supper.

I wish you would ask Ben Smith will he have
a hack down to the deepo to meet us but I won't
pay no more than $.25 and I should think he
should ought to be glad to take us from the deepo
to your house for nothing.

Your pal,   JACK.

P. S.   The train we are comeing on leaves here
at noon Al and will probily get us there in time
for a late supper and I wonder if Bertha would
have spair ribs and crout for supper. You know
me Al.

CHAPTER

6

The Busher Beats It Hence

Chicago, Ill., Oct. 18.

FRIEND AL: I guess may be you will begin
to think I dont never do what I am going to
do and that I change my mind a hole lot because
I wrote and told you that I and Florrie and little
Al would be in Bedford to-day and here we are
in Chi yet on the day when I told you we would
get to Bedford and I bet Bertha and you and the
rest of the boys will be dissapointed but Al I dont
feel like as if I should ought to leave the White
Sox in a hole and that is why I am here yet and
I will tell you how it come off but in the 1st place
I want to tell you that it wont make a diffrence
of more then 5 or 6 or may be 7 days at least and
we will be down there and see you and Bertha and
the rest of the boys just as soon as the N. Y. giants
and the White Sox leaves here and starts a round
the world. All so I remember I told you to fix
it up so as a hack would be down to the deepo
to meet us to-night and you wont get this letter

in time to tell them not to send no hack so I supose the hack will be there but may be they will be some body else that gets off of the train that will want the hack and then every thing will be all O. K. but if they is not nobody else that wants the hack I will pay them ½ of what they was going to charge me if I had of came and road in the hack though I dont have to pay them nothing because I am not going to ride in the hack but I want to do the right thing and besides I will want a hack at the deepo when I do come so they will get a peace of money out of me any way so I dont see where they got no kick comeing even if I dont give them a nichol now.

I will tell you why I am still here and you will see where I am trying to do the right thing. You knowed of coarse that the White Sox and the N. Y. giants was going to make a trip a round the world and they been after me for a long time to go a long with them but I says No I would not leave Florrie and the kid because that would not be fare and besides I would be paying rent and grocerys for them some wheres and me not getting nothing out of it and besides I would probily be spending a hole lot of money on the trip because though the clubs pays all of our regular expences they would be a hole lot of times when I felt

like blowing my self and buying some thing to
send home to the Mrs and to good old friends of
mine like you and Bertha so I turned them down
and Callahan acted like he was sore at me but I
dont care nothing for that because I got other
people to think a bout and not Callahan and besides if I was to go a long the fans in the towns
where we play at would want to see me work and
I would have to do a hole lot of pitching which
I would not be getting nothing for it and it would
not count in no standing because the games is to
be just for fun and what good would it do me
and besides Florrie says I was not under no
circumstance to go and of coarse I would go if I
wanted to go no matter what ever she says but
all and all I turned them down and says I would
stay here all winter or rather I would not stay
here but in Bedford.   Then Callahan says All
right but you know before we start on the trip
the giants and us is going to play a game right
here in Chi next Sunday and after what you done
in the city serious the fans would be sore if they
did not get no more chance to look at you so will
you stay and pitch part of the game here and I
says I would think it over and I come home to the
hotel where we are staying at and asked Florrie
did she care if we did not go to Bedford for an

other week and she says No she did not care if we
dont go for 6 years so I called Callahan up and
says I would stay and he says Thats the boy and
now the fans will have an other treat so you see
Al he appresiates what I done and wants to give
the fans fare treatment because this town is nuts
over me after what I done to them Cubs but I
could do it just the same to the Athaletics or any
body else if it would of been them in stead of the
Cubs. May be we will leave here the A. M. after
the game that is Monday and I will let you know
so as you can order an other hack and tell Bertha
I hope she did not go to no extra trouble a bout
getting ready for us and did not order no spair
ribs and crout but you can eat them up if she all
ready got them and may be she can order some
more for us when we come but tell her it dont
make no diffrence and not to go to no trouble because most anything she has is O. K. for I and
Florrie accept of coarse we would not want to
make no meal off of sardeens or something.

Well Al I bet them N. Y. giants will wish
I would of went home before they come for this
here exibishun game because my arm feels grate
and I will show them where they would be at if
they had to play ball in our league all the time
though I supose they is some pitchers in our league

that they would hit good against them if they can
hit at all but not me. You will see in the papers
how I come out and I will write and tell you a
bout it. Your pal, Jack.

Chicago, Ill., Oct. 25.

Old Pal: I have not only got a little time but
I have got some news for you and I knowed you
would want to hear all a bout it so I am writeing
this letter and then I am going to catch the train.
I would be saying good by to little Al instead of
writeing this letter only Florrie wont let me wake
him up and he is a sleep but may be by the time I
get this letter wrote he will be a wake again and
I can say good by to him. I am going with the
White Sox and giants as far as San Francisco or
may be Van Coover where they take the boat at
but I am not going a round the world with them
but only just out to the coast to help them out
because they is a couple of men going to join them
out there and untill them men join them they will
be short of men and they got a hole lot of exibishun games to play before they get out there so I
am going to help them out. It all come off in the
club house after the game to-day and I will tell
you how it come off but 1st I want to tell you a
bout the game and honest Al them giants is the

luckyest team in the world and it is not no wonder
they keep wining the penant in that league because a club that has got there luck could win ball
games with out sending no team on the field at
all but staying down to the hotel.

They was a big crowd out to the park so Callahan says to me I did not know if I was going to
pitch you or not but the crowd is out here to see
you so I will have to let you work so I warmed
up but I knowed the minute I throwed the 1st ball
warming up that I was not right and I says to
Callahan I did not feel good but he says You
wont need to feel good to beat this bunch because
they heard a hole lot a bout you and you
would have them beat if you just throwed your
glove out there in the box. So I went in and
tried to pitch but my arm was so lame it pretty
near killed me every ball I throwed and I bet if
I was some other pitchers they would not never
of tried to work with my arm so sore but I am
not like some of them yellow dogs and quit because I would not dissapoint the crowd or throw
Callahan down when he wanted me to pitch and
was depending on me. You know me Al. So I
went in there but I did not have nothing and if
them giants could of hit at all in stead of like a
lot of girls they would of knock down the fence

because I was not my self. At that they should
not ought to of had only the 1 run off of me if
Weaver and them had not of begin kicking the
ball a round like it was a foot ball or something.
Well Al what with dropping fly balls and booting
them a round and this in that the giants was gave
5 runs in the 1st 3 innings and they should ought
to of had just the 1 run or may be not that and
that ball Merkle hit in to the seats I was trying
to waist it and a man that is a good hitter would
not never of hit at it and if I was right this here
Merkle could not foul me in 9 years. When I
was comeing into the bench after the 3th inning
this here smart alex Mcgraw come passed me from
the 3 base coaching line and he says Are you going
on the trip and I says No I am not going on no
trip and he says That is to bad because if you
was going we would win a hole lot of games and
I give him a hot come back and he did not say
nothing so I went in to the bench and Callahan
says Them giants is not such rotten hitters is they
and I says No they hit pretty good when a man
has got a sore arm against them and he says Why
did not you tell me your arm was sore and I says
I did not want to dissapoint no crowd that come
out here to see me and he says Well I guess you
need not pitch no more because if I left you in

there the crowd might begin to get tired of watching you a bout 10 oclock to-night and I says What do you mean and he did not say nothing more so I set there a while and then went to the club house. Well Al after the game Callahan come in to the club house and I was still in there yet talking to the trainer and getting my arm rubbed and Callahan says Are you getting your arm in shape for next year and I says No but it give me so much pane I could not stand it and he says I bet if you was feeling good you could make them giants look like a sucker and I says You know I could make them look like a sucker and he says Well why dont you come a long with us and you will get an other chance at them when you feel good and I says I would like to get an other crack at them but I could not go a way on no trip and leave the Mrs and the baby and then he says he would not ask me to make the hole trip a round the world but he wisht I would go out to the coast with them because they was hard up for pitchers and he says Mathewson of the giants was not only going as far as the coast so if the giants had there star pitcher that far the White Sox should ought to have theren and then some of the other boys coaxed me would I go so finely I says I would think it over and I went home and seen Florrie and she says How long would it be for and I says a bout 3 or 4 weeks and she says If you dont go will we start for Bedford right a way and I says Yes and then she says All right go a head and go but if they was any thing should happen to the baby while I was gone what would they do if I was not a round to tell them what to do and I says Call a Dr. in but dont call no Dr. if you dont have to and besides you should ought to know by this time what to do for the baby when he got sick and she says Of coarse I know a little but not as much as you do because you know it all. Then I says No I dont know it all but I will tell you some things before I go and you should not ought to have no trouble so we fixed it up and her and little Al is to stay here in the hotel untill I come back which will be a bout the 20 of Nov. and then we will come down home and tell Bertha not to get to in patient and we will get there some time.   It is going to cost me $6.00 a week at the hotel for a room for she and the baby besides there meals but the babys meals dont cost nothing yet and Florrie should not ought to be very hungry because we been liveing good and besides she will get all she can eat when we come to Bedford and it wont cost me nothing for meals on the trip out to the coast because Comiskey and Mcgraw pays for that.

I have not even had no time to look up where we play at but we stop off at a hole lot of places on the way and I will get a chance to make them giants look like a sucker before I get threw and Mcgraw wont be so sorry I am not going to make the hole trip. You will see by the papers what I done to them before we get threw and I will write as soon as we stop some wheres long enough so as I can write and now I am going to say good by to little Al if he is a wake or not a wake and wake him up and say good by to him because even if he is not only 5 months old he is old enough to think a hole lot of me and why not. I all so got to say good by to Florrie and fix it up with the hotel clerk a bout she and the baby staying here a while and catch the train. You will hear from me soon old pal.

Your pal,   JACK.

St. Joe, Miss., Oct. 29.

FRIEND AL: Well Al we are on our way to the coast and they is quite a party of us though it is not no real White Sox and giants at all but some players from off of both clubs and then some others that is from other clubs a round the

2 leagues to fill up. We got Speaker from the
Boston club and Crawford from the Detroit club
and if we had them with us all the time Al I
would not never loose a game because one or the
other of them 2 is good for a couple of runs every
game and that is all I need to win my games is a
couple of runs or only 1 run and I would win
all my games and would not never loose a game.

I did not pitch to-day and I guess the giants
was glad of it because no matter what Mcgraw
says he must of saw from watching me Sunday
that I was a real pitcher though my arm was so
sore I could not hardly raze it over my sholder
so no wonder I did not have no stuff but at that
I could of beat his gang with out no stuff if I
had of had some kind of decent suport. I will
pitch against them may be to-morrow or may be
some day soon and my arm is all O. K. again
now so I will show them up and make them wish
Callahan had of left me to home. Some of the
men has brung there wife a long and besides that
there is some other men and there wife that is
not no ball players but are going a long for the
trip and some more will join the party out the
coast before they get a bord the boat but of
coarse I and Mathewson will drop out of the party
then because why should I or him go a round the

world and throw our arms out pitching games that dont count in no standing and that we dont get no money for pitching them out side of just our bare expences. The people in the towns we played at so far has all wanted to shake hands with Mathewson and I so I guess they know who is the real pitchers on these here 2 clubs no matter what them reporters says and the stars is all ways the men that the people wants to shake there hands with and make friends with them but Al this here Mathewson pitched to-day and honest Al I dont see how he gets by and either the batters in the National league dont know nothing a bout hitting or else he is such a old man that they feel sorry for him and may be when he was a bout 10 years younger then he is may be then he had some thing and was a pretty fare pitcher but all as he does now is stick the 1st ball right over with o on it and pray that they dont hit it out of the park. If a pitcher like he can get by in the National league and fool them batters they is not nothing I would like better then to pitch in the National league and I bet I would not get scored on in 2 to 3 years. I heard a hole lot a bout this here fade a way that he is suposed to pitch and it is a ball that is throwed out between 2 fingers and falls in at a right hand batter and they is not

no body cant hit it but if he throwed 1 of them
things to-day he done it while I was a sleep and
they was not no time when I was not wide a wake
and looking right at him and after the game was
over I says to him Where is that there fade a way
I heard so much a bout and he says O I did not
have to use none of my regular stuff against your
club and I says Well you would have to use all
you got if I was working against you and he says
Yes if you worked like you done Sunday I would
have to do some pitching or they would not never
finish the game. Then I says a bout me haveing
a sore arm Sunday and he says I wisht I had a
sore arm like yourn and a little sence with it and
was your age and I would not never loose a game
so you see Al he has heard a bout me and is jellus
because he has not got my stuff but they cant
every body expect to have the stuff that I got or
½ as much stuff. This smart alex Mcgraw was
trying to kid me to-day and says Why did not I
make friends with Mathewson and let him learn
me some thing a bout pitching and I says Mathewson could not learn me nothing and he says I guess
thats right and I guess they is not nobody could
learn you nothing a bout nothing and if you was
to stay in the league 20 years probily you would
not be no better then you are now so you see he

had to add mit that I am good Al even if he has
not saw me work when my arm was O. K.

Mcgraw says to me to-night he says I wisht you
was going all the way and I says Yes you do. I
says Your club would look like a sucker after I
had worked against them a few times and he says
May be thats right to because they would not
know how to hit against a regular pitcher after
that. Then he says But I dont care nothing a
bout that but I wisht you was going to make the
hole trip so as we could have a good time. He
says We got Steve Evans and Dutch Schaefer
going a long and they is both of them funny but
I like to be a round with boys that is funny and
dont know nothing a bout it. I says Well I would
go a long only for my wife and baby and he says
Yes it would be pretty tough on your wife to have
you a way that long but still and all think how
glad she would be to see you when you come back
again and besides them dolls acrost the ocean will
be pretty sore at I and Callahan if we tell them
we left you to home. I says Do you supose the
people over there has heard a bout me and he
says Sure because they have wrote a lot of letters
asking me to be sure and bring you and Mathewson a long. Then he says I guess Mathewson is not
going so if you was to go and him left here to

home they would not be nothing to it. You could have things all your own way and probily could marry the Queen of europe if you was not all ready married. He was giveing me the strate dope this time Al because he did not crack a smile and I wisht I could go a long but it would not be fare to Florrie but still and all did not she leave me and beat it for Texas last winter and why should not I do the same thing to her only I am not that kind of a man. You know me Al.

We play in Kansas city to-morrow and may be I will work there because it is a big town and I have got to close now and write to Florrie.

Your old pal,   JACK.

Abilene, Texas, Nov. 4.

AL: Well Al I guess you know by this time that I have worked against them 2 times since I wrote to you last time and I beat them both times and Mcgraw knows now what kind of a pitcher I am and I will tell you how I know because after the game yesterday he road down to the place we dressed at a long with me and all the way in the automobile he was after me to say I would go all the way a round the world and finely it come out that he wants I should go a long and pitch for his club and not pitch for the White Sox. He says

his club is up against it for pitchers because
Mathewson is not going and all they got left is
a man named Hern that is a young man and not
got no experiense and Wiltse that is a left hander.
So he says I have talked it over with Callahan
and he says if I could get you to go a long it was
all O. K. with him and you could pitch for us
only I must not work you to hard because he is
depending on you to win the penant for him next
year. I says Did not none of the other White
Sox make no holler because may be they might
have to bat against me and he says Yes Crawford
and Speaker says they would not make the trip
if you was a long and pitching against them but
Callahan showed them where it would be good
for them next year because if they hit against you
all winter the pitchers they hit against next year
will look easy to them. He was crazy to have me
go a long on the hole trip but of coarse Al they
is not no chance of me going on acct. of Florrie
and little Al but you see Mcgraw has cut out his
trying to kid me and is treating me now like a
man should ought to be treated that has did what
I done.

They was not no game here to-day on acct. of it
raining and the people here was sore because they
did not see no game but they all come a round

to look at us and says they must have some speechs from the most prommerent men in the party so I and Comiskey and Mcgraw and Callahan and Mathewson and Ted Sullivan that I guess is putting up the money for the trip made speechs and they clapped there hands harder when I was makeing my speech then when any 1 of the others was makeing there speech. You did not know I was a speech maker did you Al and I did not know it neither untill to-day but I guess they is not nothing I can do if I make up my mind and 1 of the boys says that I done just as well as Dummy Taylor could of.

I have not heard nothing from Florrie but I guess may be she is to busy takeing care of little Al to write no letters and I am not worring none because she give me her word she would let me know was they some thing the matter.

Yours truly,   JACK.

San Dago, Cal., Nov. 9.

FRIEND AL: Al some times I wisht I was not married at all and if it was not for Florrie and little Al I would go a round the world on this here trip and I guess the boys in Bedford would not be jellus if I was to go a round the world and see every thing they is to be saw and some of the

boys down home has not never been no futher a
way then Terre Haute and I dont mean you Al
but some of the other boys. But of coarse Al
when a man has got a wife and a baby they is not
no chance for him to go a way on 1 of these here
trips and leave them a lone so they is not no use
I should even think a bout it but I cant help
thinking a bout it because the boys keeps after me
all the time to go. Callahan was talking a bout
it to me to-day and he says he knowed that if I
was to pitch for the giants on the trip his club
would not have no chance of wining the most of
the games on the trip but still and all he wisht I
would go a long because he was a scared the people over in Rome and Paris and Africa and them
other countrys would be awful sore if the 2 clubs
come over there with out bringing none of there
star pitchers along. He says We got Speaker
and Crawford and Doyle and Thorp and some of
them other real stars in all the positions accept
pitcher and it will make us look bad if you and
Mathewson dont neither 1 of you come a long. I
says What is the matter with Scott and Benz and
this here left hander Wiltse and he says They
is not nothing the matter with none of them accept they is not no real stars like you and Mathewson and if we cant show them forreners 1 of you

2 we will feel like as if we was cheating them. I says You would not want me to pitch my best against your club would you and he says O no I would not want you to pitch your best or get your self all wore out for next year but I would want you to let up enough so as we could make a run oncet in a while so the games would not be to 1 sided. I says Well they is not no use talking a bout it because I could not leave my wife and baby and he says Why dont you write and ask your wife and tell her how it is and can you go. I says No because she would make a big holler and besides of coarse I would go any way if I wanted to go with out no I yes or no from her only I am not the kind of a man that runs off and leaves his family and besides they is not nobody to leave her with because her and her sister Allens wife has had a quarrle. Then Callahan says Where is Allen at now is he still in Chi. I says I dont know where is he at and I dont care where he is at because I am threw with him. Then Callahan says I asked him would he go on the trip before the season was over but he says he could not and if I knowed where was he I would wire a telegram to him and ask him again. I says What would you want him a long for and he says Because Mcgraw is shy of pitchers and I says I

would try and help him find 1. I says Well you should ought not to have no trouble finding a man like Allen to go along because his wife probily would be glad to get rid of him. Then Callahan says Well I wisht you would get a hold of where Allen is at and let me know so as I can wire him a telegram. Well Al I know where Allen is at all O. K. but I am not going to give his adress to Callahan because Mcgraw has treated me all O. K. and why should I wish a man like Allen on to him and besides I am not going to give Allen no chance to go a round the world or no wheres else after the way he acted a bout I and Florrie haveing a room in his flat and asking me to pay for it when he give me a invatation to come there and stay. Well Al it is to late now to cry in the sour milk but I wisht I had not never saw Florrie untill next year and then I and her could get married just like we done last year only I dont know would I do it again or not but I guess I would on acct. of little Al.

Your pal, JACK.

San Francisco, Cal., Nov. 14.

OLD PAL: Well old pal what do you know a bout me being back here in San Francisco where I give the fans such a treat 2 years ago and then

I was not nothing but a busher and now I am
with a team that is going a round the world and
are crazy to have me go a long only I cant because of my wife and baby. Callahan wired a
telegram to the reporters here from Los Angeles
telling them I would pitch here and I guess they
is going to be 20 or 25000 out to the park and I
will give them the best I got.

But what do you think Florrie has did Al. Her
and the Allens has made it up there quarrle and
is friends again and Marie told Florrie to write
and tell me she was sorry we had that there argument and let by gones be by gones. Well Al it
is all O. K. with me because I cant help not feeling sorry for Allen because I dont beleive he will
be in the league next year and I feel sorry for
Marie to because it must be pretty tough on her
to see how well her sister done and what a miss-
take she made when she went and fell for a left
hander that could not fool a blind man with his
curve ball and if he was to hit a man in the head
with his fast ball they would think there nose
iched. In Florries letter she says she thinks us
and the Allens could find an other flat like the 1
we had last winter and all live in it to gether in
stead of going to Bedford but I have wrote to
her before I started writeing this letter all ready

and told her that her and I is going to Bedford
and the Allens can go where they feel like and
they can go and stay on a boat on Michigan lake
all winter if they want to but I and Florrie is
comeing to Bedford. Down to the bottom of her
letter she says Allen wants to know if Callahan
or Mcgraw is shy of pitchers and may be he would
change his mind and go a long on the trip. Well
Al I did not ask either Callahan nor Mcgraw
nothing a bout it because I knowed they was looking for a star and not for no left hander that
could not brake a pane of glass with his fast 1 so
I wrote and told Florrie to tell Allen they was all
filled up and would not have no room for no more
men.

It is pretty near time to go out to the ball park
and I wisht you could be here Al and hear them
San Francisco fans go crazy when they hear my
name anounced to pitch. I bet they wish they
had of had me here this last year.

Yours truly,   JACK.

Medford, Organ, Nov. 16.

FRIEND AL: Well Al you know by this time
that I did not pitch the hole game in San Francisco but I was not tooken out because they was
hitting me Al but because my arm went back on

me all of a sudden and it was the change in the
clime it that done it to me and they could not hire
me to try and pitch another game in San Francisco. They was the biggest crowd there that I
ever seen in San Francisco and I guess they must
of been 40000 people there and I wisht you could
of heard them yell when my name was anounced
to pitch. But Al I would not never of went in
there but for the crowd. My arm felt like a wet
rag or some thing and I knowed I would not have
nothing and besides the people was packed in a
round the field and they had to have ground rules
so when a man hit a pop fly it went in to the
crowd some wheres and was a 2 bagger and all
them giants could do against me was pop my fast
ball up in the air and then the wind took a hold
of it and dropped it in to the crowd the lucky
stiffs.   Doyle hit 3 of them pop ups in to the
crowd so when you see them 3 2 base hits oposit
his name in the score you will know they was not
no real 2 base hits and the infielders would of
catched them had it not of been for the wind.
This here Doyle takes a awful wallop at a ball
but if I was right and he swang at a ball the way
he done in San Francisco the catcher would all
ready be throwing me back the ball a bout the
time this here Doyle was swinging at it.   I can

make him look like a sucker and I done it both in
Kansas city and Bonham and if he will get up
there and bat against me when I feel good and
when they is not no wind blowing I will bet him
a $25.00 suit of cloths that he cant foul 1 off of
me. Well when Callahan seen how bad my arm
was he says I guess I should ought to take you out
and not run no chance of you getting killed in
there and so I quit and Faber went in to finnish
it up because it dont make no diffrence if he hurts
his arm or dont. But I guess Mcgraw knowed
my arm was sore to because he did not try and kid
me like he done that day in Chi because he has
saw enough of me since then to know I can make
his club look rotten when I am O.K. and my arm
is good. On the train that night he come up and
says to me Well Jack we catched you off your
strid to-day or you would of gave us a beating
and then he says What your arm needs is more
work and you should ought to make the hole trip
with us and then you would be in fine shape for
next year but I says You cant get me to make no
trip so you might is well not do no more talking
a bout it and then he says Well I am sorry and
the girls over to Paris will be sorry to but I guess
he was just jokeing a bout the last part of it.

Well Al we go to 1 more town in Organ and

then to Washington but of coarse it is not the same
Washington we play at in the summer but this
is the state Washington and have not got no big
league club and the boys gets there boat in 4 more
days and I will quit them and then I will come
strate back to Chi and from there to Bedford.

     Your pal,   JACK.

      Portland, Organ, Nov. 17.

  FRIEND AL: I have just wrote a long letter
to Florrie but I feel like as if I should ought to
write to you because I wont have no more chance
for a long while that is I wont have no more
chance to male a letter because I will be on the
pacific Ocean and un less we should run passed a
boat that was comeing the other way they would
not be no chance of getting no letter maled. Old
pal I am going to make the hole trip clear a round
the world and back and so I wont see you this
winter after all but when I do see you Al I will
have a lot to tell you a bout my trip and besides
I will write you a letter a bout it from every place
we head in at.

  I guess you will be surprised a bout me changeing my mind and makeing the hole trip but they
was not no way for me to get out of it and I will
tell you how it all come off. While we was still

in that there Medford yesterday Mcgraw and Callahan come up to me and says was they not no
chance of me changeing my mind a bout makeing
the hole trip. I says No they was not. Then
Callahan says Well I dont know what we are
going to do then and I says Why and he says
Comiskey just got a letter from president Wilson
the President of the united states and in the letter
president Wilson says he had got an other letter
from the king of Japan who says that they would
not stand for the White Sox and giants comeing
to Japan un less they brought all there stars a long
and president Wilson says they would have to
take there stars a long because he was a scared
if they did not take there stars a long Japan would
get mad at the united states and start a war and
then where would we be at. So Comiskey wired
a telegram to president Wilson and says Mathewson could not make the trip because he was so
old but would everything be all O.K. if I was to
go a long and president Wilson wired a telegram
back and says Yes he had been talking to the
priest from Japan and he says Yes it would be
all O.K. I asked them would they show me the
letter from president Wilson because I thought
may be they might be kiding me and they says
they could not show me no letter because when

Comiskey got the letter he got so mad that he tore it up. Well Al I finely says I did not want to brake up there trip but I knowed Florrie would not stand for letting me go so Callahan says All right I will wire a telegram to a friend of mine in Chi and have him get a hold of Allen and send him out here and we will take him a long and I says It is to late for Allen to get here in time and Mcgraw says No they was a train that only took 2 days from Chi to where ever it was the boat is going to sale from because the train come a round threw canada and it was down hill all the way. Then I says Well if you will wire a telegram to my wife and fix things up with her I will go a long with you but if she is going to make a holler it is all off. So we all 3 went to the telegram office to gether and we wired Florrie a telegram that must of cost $2.00 but Callahan and Mcgraw payed for it out of there own pocket and then we waited a round a long time and the anser come back and the anser was longer than the telegram we wired and it says it would not make no diffrence to her but she did not know if the baby would make a holler but he was hollering most of the time any way so that would not make no diffrence but if she let me go it was on condishon that her and the Allens could get a flat to gether

and stay in Chi all winter and not go to no Bedford and hire a nurse to take care of the baby
and if I would send her a check for the money I
had in the bank so as she could put it in her name
and draw it out when she need it. Well I says
at 1st I would not stand for nothing like that but
Callahan and Mcgraw showed me where I was
makeing a mistake not going when I could see all
them diffrent countrys and tell Florrie all a bout
the trip when I come back and then in a year or
2 when the baby was a little older I could make
an other trip and take little Al and Florrie a long
so I finely says O.K. I would go and we wires
still an other telegram to Florrie and told her
O.K. and then I set down and wrote her a check
for ½ the money I got in the bank and I got
$500.00 all together there so I wrote the check
for ½ of that or $250.00 and maled it to her
and if she cant get a long on that she would be
a awfull spendrift because I am not only going
to be a way untill March. You should ought to
of heard the boys cheer when Callahan tells them
I am going to make the hole trip but when he tells
them I am going to pitch for the giants and not
for the White Sox I bet Crawford and Speaker
and them wisht I was going to stay to home but

it is just like Callahan says if they bat against me
all winter the pitchers they bat against next season will look easy to them and you wont be supprised Al if Crawford and Speaker hits a bout 500
next year and if they hit good you will know
why it is. Steve Evans asked me was I all fixed
up with cloths and I says No but I was going
out and buy some cloths includeing a full dress
suit of evening cloths and he says You dont need
no full dress suit of evening cloths because you
look funny enough with out them. This Evans
is a great kidder Al and no body never gets sore
at the stuff he pulls some thing like Kid Gleason.
I wisht Kid Gleason was going on the trip Al but
I will tell him all a bout it when I come back.

Well Al old pal I wisht you was going a long
to and I bet we could have the time of our life
but I will write to you right a long Al and I will
send Bertha some post cards from the diffrent
places we head in at. I will try and write you
a letter on the boat and male it as soon as we get
to the 1st station which is either Japan or Yoko-
hama I forgot which. Good by Al and say good
by to Bertha for me and tell her how sorry I and
Florrie is that we cant come to Bedford this winter but we will spend all the rest of the winters

there and her and Florrie will have a plenty of
time to get acquainted. Good by old pal.

Your pal,   JACK.

Seattle, Wash., Nov. 18.

AL: Well Al it is all off and I am not going
on no trip a round the world and back and I been
looking for Callahan or Mcgraw for the last ½
hour to tell them I have changed my mind and
am not going to make no trip because it would
not be fare to Florrie and besides that I think I
should ought to stay home and take care of little
Al and not leave him to be tooken care of by no
train nurse because how do I know what would
she do to him and I am not going to tell Florrie
nothing a bout it but I am going to take the train
to-morrow night right back to Chi and supprise
her when I get there and I bet both her and little
Al will be tickled to death to see me. I supose
Mcgraw and Callahan will be sore at me for a
while but when I tell them I want to do the right
thing and not give my famly no raw deal I guess
they will see where I am right.

We was to play 2 games here and was to play
1 of them in Tacoma and the other here but it
rained and so we did not play neither 1 and the
people was pretty mad a bout it because I was an-

nounced to pitch and they figured probily this would be there only chance to see me in axion and they made a awful holler but Comiskey says No they would not be no game because the field neither here or in Tacoma was in no shape for a game and he would not take no chance of me pitching and may be slipping in the mud and straneing myself and then where would the White Sox be at next season. So we been laying a round all the P.M. and I and Dutch Schaefer had a long talk to gether while some of the rest of the boys was out buying some cloths to take on the trip and Al I bought a full dress suit of evening cloths at Portland yesterday and now I owe Callahan the money for them and am not going on no trip so probily I wont never get to ware them and it is just $45.00 throwed a way but I would rather throw $45.00 a way then go on a trip a round the world and leave my famly all winter.

Well Al I and Schaefer was talking to gether and he says Well may be this is the last time we will ever see the good old US and I says What do you mean and he says People that gos acrost the pacific Ocean most generally all ways has there ship recked and then they is not no more never heard from them. Then he asked me was I a good swimmer and I says Yes I had swam a good deal

in the river and he says Yes you have swam in
the river but that is not nothing like swimming
in the pacific Ocean because when you swim in
the pacific Ocean you cant move your feet because
if you move your feet the sharks comes up to the
top of the water and bites at them and even if
they did not bite your feet clean off there bite
is poison and gives you the hiderofobeya and when
you get that you start barking like a dog and the
water runs in to your mouth and chokes you to
death.   Then he says Of coarse if you can swim
with out useing your feet you are all O.K. but
they is very few can do that and especially in the
pacific Ocean because they got to keep useing there
hands all the time to scare the sord fish a way so
when you dont dare use your feet and your hands
is busy you got nothing left to swim with but your
stumach mussles.   Then he says You should ought
to get a long all O.K. because your stumach mussles should ought to be strong from the exercise
they get so I guess they is not no danger from
a man like you but men like Wiltse and Mike
Donlin that is not hog fat like you has not got
no chance.   Then he says Of coarse they have
been times when the boats got acrost all O.K. and
only a few lives lost but it dont offten happen
and the time the old Minneapolis club made the

trip the boat went down and the only thing that
was saved was the catchers protector that was
full of air and could not do nothing else but
flote. Then he says May be you would flote to
if you did not say nothing for a few days.

I asked him how far would a man got to swim
if some thing went wrong with the boat and he
says O not far because they is a hole lot of ilands
a long the way that a man could swim to but it
would not do a man no good to swim to these here
ilands because they dont have nothing to eat on
them and a man would probily starve to death
un less he happened to swim to the sandwich
ilands. Then he says But by the time you been
out on the pacific Ocean a few months you wont
care if you get any thing to eat or not. I says
Why not and he says the pacific Ocean is so ruff
that not nothing can set still not even the stuff
you eat. I asked him how long did it take to
make the trip acrost if they was not no ship reck
and he says they should ought to get acrost a
long in febuery if the weather was good. I says
Well if we dont get there until febuery we wont
have no time to train for next season and he says
You wont need to do no training because this trip
will take all the weight off of you and every thing
else you got. Then he says But you should not

ought to be scared of getting sea sick because they
is 1 way you can get a way from it and that is
to not eat nothing at all while you are on the
boat and they tell me you dont eat hardly nothing
any way so you wont miss it. Then he says Of
coarse if we should have good luck and not get in
to no ship reck and not get shot by 1 of them
war ships we will have a grate time when we get
acrost because all the girls in europe and them
places is nuts over ball players and especially stars.
I asked what did he mean saying we might get
shot by 1 of them war ships and he says we would
have to pass by Swittserland and the Swittserland
war ships was all the time shooting all over the
ocean and of coarse they was not trying to hit no
body but they was as wild as most of them left
handers and how could you tell what was they
going to do next.

Well Al after I got threw talking to Schaefer
I run in to Jack Sheridan the umpire and I says
I did not think I would go on no trip and I told
him some of the things Schaefer was telling me
and Sheridan says Schaefer was kidding me and
they was not no danger at all and of coarse Al I
did not believe ½ of what Schaefer was telling
me and that has not got nothing to do with me
changeing my mind but I don't think it is not

hardly fare for me to go a way on a trip like that and leave Florrie and the baby and suppose some of them things really did happen like Schaefer said though of coarse he was kidding me but if 1 of them was to happen they would not be no body left to take care of Florrie and little Al and I got a $1000.00 insurence policy but how do I know after I am dead if the insurence co. comes acrost and gives my famly the money.

Well Al I will male this letter and then try again and find Mcgraw and Callahan and then I will look up a time table and see what train can I get to Chi. I dont know yet when I will be in Bedford and may be Florrie has hired a flat all ready but the Allens can live in it by them self and if Allen says any thing a bout I paying for ½ of the rent I will bust his jaw.

Your pal,   JACK.

Victoria, Can., Nov. 19.

DEAR OLD AL: Well old pal the boat gos to-night I am going a long and I would not be takeing no time to write this letter only I wrote to you yesterday and says I was not going and you probily would be expecting to see me blow in to Bedford in a few days and besides Al I got a hole lot of things to ask you to do for me if any thing happens and I want to tell you how it come a bout that I changed my mind and am going on the trip. I am glad now that I did not write Florrie no letter yesterday and tell her I was not going because now I would have to write her an other letter and tell her I was going and she would be expecting to see me the day after she got the 1st letter and in stead of seeing me she would get this 2nd. letter and not me at all. I have all ready wrote her a good by letter to-day though and while I was writeing it Al I all most broke down and cried and espesially when I thought a bout leaveing little Al so long and may be when I see him again he wont be no baby no more or may be some thing will of happened to him or that train nurse did some thing to him or may be I wont never see him again no more because it is pretty near a cinch that some thing will either happen to I or him. I would give all most any thing I got Al to be back in Chi with little Al and Florrie and I wisht she had not of never wired that telegram telling me I could make the trip and if some thing happens to me think how she will feel when ever she thinks a bout wireing me that telegram and she will feel all most like as if she was a murder.

Well Al after I had wrote you that letter yesterday I found Callahan and Mcgraw and I tell them I have changed my mind and am not going on no trip. Callahan says Whats the matter and I says I dont think it would be fare to my wife and baby and Callahan says Your wife says it would be all O.K. because I seen the telegram my self. I says Yes but she dont know how dangerus the trip is and he says Whos been kiding you and I says They has not no body been kiding me. I says Dutch Schaefer told me a hole lot of stuff but I did not believe none of it and that has not got nothing to do with it. I says I am not a scared of nothing but supose some thing should happen and then where would my wife and my baby be at. Then Callahan says Schaefer has been giveing you a lot of hot air and they is not no more danger on this trip then they is in bed. You been in a hole lot more danger when you was pitching some of them days when you had a sore arm and you would be takeing more chances of getting killed in Chi by 1 of them taxi cabs or the dog catcher then on the Ocean. This here boat we are going on is the Umpires of Japan and it has went acrost the Ocean a million times with out nothing happening and they could not nothing happen to a boat that the N. Y. giants was rideing on because they is to lucky. Then I

says Well I have made up my mind to not go on
no trip and he says All right then I guess we might
is well call the trip off and I says Why and he
says You know what president Wilson says a bout
Japan and they wont stand for us comeing over
there with out you a long and then Mcgraw says
Yes it looks like as if the trip was off because
we dont want to take no chance of starting no
war between Japan and the united states. Then
Callahan says You will be in fine with Comiskey
if he has to call the trip off because you are a
scared of getting hit by a fish. Well Al we talked
and argude for a hour or a hour and ½ and some
of the rest of the boys come a round and took Callahan and Mcgraw side and finely Callahan says
it looked like as if they would have to posepone
the trip a few days untill he could get a hold of
Allen or some body and get them to take my place
so finely I says I would go because I would not
want to brake up no trip after they had made all
there plans and some of the players wifes was all
ready to go and would be dissapointed if they was
not no trip. So Mcgraw and Callahan says Thats
the way to talk and so I am going Al and we are
leaveing to-night and may be this is the last letter
you will ever get from me but if they does not
nothing happen Al I will write to you a lot of

letters and tell you all a bout the trip but you
must not be looking for no more letters for a while
untill we get to Japan where I can male a letter
and may be its likely as not we wont never get
to Japan.

Here is the things I want to ask you to try
and do Al and I am not asking you to do nothing
if we get threw the trip all right but if some thing
happens and I should be drowned here is what I
am asking you to do for me and that is to see that
the insurence co. dont skin Florrie out of that
$1000.00 policy and see that she all so gets that
other $250.00 out of the bank and find her some
place down in Bedford to live if she is willing to
live down there because she can live there a hole
lot cheaper then she can live in Chi and besides
I know Bertha would treat her right and help
her out all she could.   All so Al I want you and
Bertha to help take care of little Al untill he grows
up big enough to take care of him self and if he
looks like as if he was going to be left handed
dont let him Al but make him use his right hand
for every thing.   Well Al they is 1 good thing
and that is if I get drowned Florrie wont have to
buy no lot in no cemetary and hire no herse.

Well Al old pal you all ways been a good friend
of mine and I all ways tried to be a good friend

of yourn and if they was ever any thing I done to you that was not O.K. remember by gones is by gones. I want you to all ways think of me as your best old pal. Good by old pal.

Your old pal,   JACK.

P.S. Al if they should not nothing happen and if we was to get acrost the Ocean all O.K. I am going to ask Mcgraw to let me work the 1st game against the White Sox in Japan because I should certainly ought to be right after giveing my arm a rest and not doing nothing at all on the trip acrost and I bet if Mcgraw lets me work Crawford and Speaker will wisht the boat had of sank. You know me Al.

PRAIRIE STATE BOOKS

Mr. Dooley in Peace
and in War
Finley Peter Dunne

Life in Prairie Land
Eliza W. Farnham

Carl Sandburg
Harry Golden

The Sangamon
Edgar Lee Masters

American Years
Harold Sinclair

The Jungle
Upton Sinclair

Twenty Years at
Hull-House
Jane Addams

They Broke the Prairie
Earnest Elmo Calkins

The Illinois
James Gray

The Valley of Shadows:
Sangamon Sketches
Francis Grierson

The Precipice
Elia W. Peattie

Across Spoon River
Edgar Lee Masters

The Rivers of Eros
Cyrus Colter

Summer on the Lakes, in 1843
Margaret Fuller

Black Hawk: An Autobiography
Edited by Donald Jackson

Wau-Bun: The "Early Day"
in the North-West
Juliette M. Kinzie

You Know Me Al
Ring W. Lardner

Chicago Poems
Carl Sandburg